Three Deep Breaths

three
deep
breaths

Finding Power and Purpose
in a Stressed-Out World

Thomas Crum

BERRETT–KOEHLER PUBLISHERS, INC.
San Francisco
a BK Life book

BERRETT-KOEHLER PUBLISHERS, INC.
235 Montgomery Street, Suite 650 San Francisco, CA 94104-2916
TEL: 415-288-0260 FAX: 415-362-2512 www.bkconnection.com

ORDERING INFORMATION
QUANTITY SALES Special discounts are available on quantity purchases by corporations, associations, and others. For details, contact the "Special Sales Department" at the Berrett-Koehler address above.
INDIVIDUAL SALES Berrett-Koehler publications are available through most bookstores. They can also be ordered directly from Berrett-Koehler:
TEL: 800-929-2929; FAX: 802-864-7626; www.bkconnection.com
ORDERS FOR COLLEGE TEXTBOOK/COURSE ADOPTION USE
Please contact Berrett-Koehler: TEL: 800-929-2929; FAX: 802-864-7626.
ORDERS BY U.S. TRADE BOOKSTORES AND WHOLESALERS
Please contact Publishers Group West, 1700 Fourth Street,
Berkeley, CA 94710. TEL: 510-528-1444; FAX: 510-528-3444.

Berrett-Koehler and the BK logo are registered trademarks of Berrett-Koehler Publishers, Inc.

Printed in the United States of America

Berrett-Koehler books are printed on long-lasting acid-free paper. When it is available, we choose paper that has been manufactured by environmentally responsible processes. These may include using trees grown in sustainable forests, incorporating recycled paper, minimizing chlorine in bleaching, or recycling the energy produced at the paper mill.

Library of Congress Cataloging-in-Publication Data
Crum, Thomas F.
    Three deep breaths : finding power and purpose in a stressed-out world / Thomas Crum.
        p. cm.
    Includes index.
    Contents: The wrinkle—The lift—The first breath—Centering—A master teacher in disguise—The second breath—Possibility—The third breath—The mystery—The journal—Practice, practice, practice.
    ISBN-10: 1-57675-389-1   ISBN-13: 978-1-57675-389-7
    1. Breathing exercises—Miscellanea. 2. Stress management—Miscellanea. 3. Respiration—Miscellanea. I. Title.

    RA782.C78 2006
    615.8'36—dc22   2005057248

FIRST EDITION
11 10 09 08 07 06   10 9 8 7 6 5 4 3 2 1

I have made every effort to locate the creator or origin of the phrase "Snowmen fall from heaven unassembled" with no luck whatsoever. This phrase is used by everyone from artists and writers to t-shirt vendors and needlepoint pattern sellers. The quote is not my own creation; I present it to readers as a beautiful and insightful piece of advice. If anyone knows, and can provide evidence of the origins or originator of the phrase, I will be more than happy to credit him or her in reprints and other editions of this book.

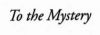

To the Mystery

Contents

Foreword

The World Health Organization has called stress a worldwide epidemic. Surveys show that 75 to 90 percent of all visits to primary care physicians are for stress-related conditions! Job stress alone is costing us a fortune. According to a report from the American Institute of Stress, U.S. businesses pay 300 billion dollars a year in job-related stress costs and *that figure is expected to rise in the future.*

Science says that stress occurs whenever a significant change happens in your mind or body, or in the environment in which you live. It could have a positive or negative source—going on a vacation or having a fight with a colleague, buying a new home or being late for an appointment. Let's face it. In this ever-changing world of increased complexity, information overload, new technologies, time crunches, and relationship struggles—*there will be stress.* As you will discover in this parable about a man crazed by the complexity of modern life, we have a choice. We can allow stress to gnaw at our minds and bodies all the way to the doctor's office, or we can see it as an opportunity to become wiser, stronger, and more flexible, like an elite athlete stressing his body in daily workouts.

Once we know we have a choice, the direction we take is obvious: health over illness, joy over frustration. A thirty-year study at Johns Hopkins University involving one thousand men found that those who got upset over everyday stresses were about three times more likely to have a heart attack and six times more likely to have a stroke than those who took life in stride. As Epictetus says, "Man is troubled not by events themselves, but by the views he takes of them."

So, how do we take a stressful life in stride? We know it can't be done just intellectually: when we are under stress or in conflict, *everything* is involved—our emotions, our bodies, our minds, our spirits. Our choices must be of a mind/body/spirit nature. Our choices must include the whole being.

Enter Tom Crum.

I first learned for myself about Tom when I heard him speak at the National Speakers Association. His unique and brilliant thinking, his energetic aikido demonstration, and his pureness of intention wowed my soul. I recognized that he was a world changer and dedicated to doing immense amounts of good. I knew from his history that he had been singer John Denver's bodyguard, mentor, and best friend. I became an instant fan, friend, student, and reader of everything that Tom did.

Tom is a seminar leader, aikido expert, and the author of two books, *The Magic of Conflict* and *Journey to Center*. Tom Crum helps people develop the total mind/body/spirit approach needed to turn stress into power and purpose.

Aikido is a Japanese form of self-defense that focuses on the energy of an attacking opponent to render his attack harmless, without doing harm, even to the attacker. "If someone goes to punch you," Tom teaches, "don't try to block the punch. When you do that, you are using resistance—your own power and strength against the attacker's. That sets up a win/lose confrontation." Tom shows people how to step aside with an accepting and pivoting movement, using the attacker's energy to throw the person or to apply a neutralizing technique. The key to all this, as Tom teaches, is to learn how to be centered and to see the bigger picture—the needs and wants of both—so that you can move to higher ground, where true solutions can be found. I have often heard Tom say, "You would not get in front of a fast-moving train. When someone comes at you in anger, step aside and try to figure out where the energy is coming from." That is one of the keys to his Magic of Conflict approach that he has shared with thousands throughout the world. Conflict isn't bad; it's an opportunity, a reminder for us to seek our higher selves.

My first real contact with Tom was participating in one of his Magic of Skiing programs. Living in Aspen, Colorado, he applies the Magic of Conflict approach to this wonderful sport. Tom teaches that skiing and snowboarding can be a magical opportunity to move to higher ground, even without the chairlifts. When you go skiing, you learn to take any challenging conditions (such as stormy weather, icy conditions, rental equipment) and turn them into a great day. He encourages you to choose your criteria for success: it's a great day because you're learning; or it's a great day because you are with friends; or it's a great day because you're breathing. I love to ski but I was really cautious and stuck in skiing as a beginner on the green slopes. Tom got me to realize that skiing was all about the use of energy. "Where is the energy going on the mountain?" he would ask. "Down the hill," everybody would answer. "Then that's where you have to send your energy. If you turn downhill but your energy is holding back, you are fighting the mountain. Instead of fighting the mountain, become one with it. Relax and go with the energy of the mountain." Tom got me breathing in as I approached a turn and breathing out as I finished a turn. I was amazed at how easily I could go down the mountain when I was concentrating on breathing and awareness, not just techniques.

As Tom would say, "Only when you are present to the energy around you can you learn to dance with life." Tom's approach is so invigorating that it not only improved my skiing, but it also improved my life. Tom is one of the world's greatest life coaches. Every morning, Tom led us in meditation, stretching, and specific exercises which centered us, made us feel awake, alive, energized, excited, ready to ski, and, better yet, ready to take on ever-bigger life challenges.

I loved skiing with Tom and the other students. It was a heartfelt joy and made me a happy ski addict. What really revealed the greatness of the man to me was when he fell on his ski pole, instantly breaking one of his ribs. Tom acknowledged the problem and his personal pain, and continued to ski and teach the rest of the day. One of the students was a doctor of acupuncture from Honolulu. Tom asked us to join him in his home for dinner that night.

Entering Tom's home is an eye-opener. It is a multilevel home with no staircases from level to level, only ropes, ladders, and bridges. Tom and his wife built it with their children in mind. It is heaven for kids and adults like me who are still kids at heart.

After dinner, the acupuncturist worked on Tom's broken rib and gave him an acupuncture treatment that started the healing process. I was delighted to see such quick results. The next morning, Tom was teaching aikido, moving and skiing as though nothing had happened. Tom is one of my heroes. He actually lives the exemplary nonconflicted life that he talks about.

Tom's parable, which you have in your hands, shows how to handle and conquer our modern epidemic of stress. But this is not a book of tips. Simply giving people advice like "eat better," "improve your work/life balance," "set priorities," "get regular exercise," and "clean up your relationship" won't do it. People are constantly hearing tips everywhere from friends, magazines, and a barrage of TV commercials trying to sell something. They have become numb to the possibility that sustained fulfillment is a reality that they actually can, with practice, integrate into their daily lives.

Tom's *Three Deep Breaths* provides us with what science says is critical in dealing with stressful living: a sense of control about how we respond to life's situations. And, best of all, it doesn't take time, you can do it anywhere, and it really works.

Tom's *Three Deep Breaths* is beguilingly simple. Simplicity doesn't mean superficial, nor does it mean instant success. Just because I'm learning the skills to be a good skier doesn't give me instant passage down the steepest mogul run on the mountain. But, as nature teaches us, simplicity and efficiency go hand in hand, and there is great beauty in being present, focused, and uncomplicated.

As I read *Three Deep Breaths,* I knew immediately that this philosophy was a wonderful strategy to help me seek the higher ground, focus on the spirit, and be the best me that I can be.

FOREWORD

Read this wonderful story about the transformation of Angus, a self-centered, task-oriented, type-A man whose tunnel vision blocked the bigger picture. On the way to work, at home, or anywhere, you can learn to use Tom's *Three Deep Breaths* to help you become more aware and connect, rather than compete, with others. You will like yourself better and everyone you contact will like you better, too.

Mark Victor Hansen

Acknowledgments

To Mark Victor Hansen, who took the time to support this work and write the foreword despite his ridiculously busy schedule of producing best-seller after best-seller!

To Ken Blanchard, for giving me the right kick in the pants at the right time to get me to put pen to paper.

To Martha Lawrence, for her insight and understanding, and for becoming a real pal to me in this process.

To Judy Warner, who is always there to assist me, doing whatever it takes, no matter how much, how difficult, and who still finds time to compassionately serve all those around her.

To Dr. Hal Bidlack, a.k.a. "Alexander Hamilton," whose humor and creativity always lift me up when I'm down in the writing trenches.

To Koichi Tohei and Rod Kobayashi, for bringing aikido and centering into my life.

To Steve Piersanti, Jeevan Sivasubramaniam, and the rest of the team at Berrett-Koehler Publishers, for showing me what a great author-publisher relationship should look like.

To Ali Crum, who has honored me with the talent and the desire to continue this work. And to all those others who gave me their valuable feedback: B. J. Adams, Amanda Boxtell, Eri Crum, Erin Crum, Tommy Crum, Jeanette Darnauer, Rio de la Vista, Richard Diehl (the acupuncturist mentioned in the foreword), Karmen Lee Dobslaff, Glenn Dutton, Graham Morrell, Judy Ringer, Ellen Stapenhorst, and Kristen Usich.

And to Cathy Crum, my brilliant editor and my best friend in the world, whose unwavering love and support show up even in her suggestions and corrections of every draft I've ever written.

Three Deep Breaths

The Wrinkle

He probably never would have looked at his reflection at all, if it hadn't been for something his daughter said. He would have done what he usually did—go downstairs, get on his computer, and wrestle with deadlines and dilemmas. But tonight, while he was tucking her into bed, Angus noticed Sierra looking at him intently.

"Why do you have that big line on your face, Daddy?"

"What big line?"

"This big line here," she said, tracing with her finger a line on his brow that extended down between his eyes.

"I guess it's from worrying too much," was Angus's truthful reply.

"What are you going to do?" his daughter persisted.

"I'm not sure."

He kissed her good night and reached to turn off the light.

"When I'm not sure of something I just ask my teacher."

"That's a good idea, Sierra. Now, go to sleep," he said, closing her bedroom door.

"And my teacher says the answers are always there, Daddy," he heard her call out. "You just have to look for them."

1

That was when he caught his reflection in the hallway mirror.

It answered back unflinchingly.

Behind that professional demeanor and that successful-looking suit, that crisply pressed shirt and silk tie, lurked something Angus didn't like. Something unnerving, like driving a car with loose brakes. The headset from his cell phone was still dangling around his neck, keeping him connected, but connected to what? He focused in on his tired eyes and the wrinkles on his brow. So this was the result of all this striving for success. Angus put both hands on the little table under the mirror to get a closer look. Sure, he had a good job, a loving wife, a wonderful eight-year-old daughter, a nice home. Wasn't he supposed to be happy? What was this miserable feeling and what was behind this sad and bewildered face?

The image didn't look at all like the person he wanted to be. He saw right through the efficient business-suit exterior to the stressed-out, "no time available" man he had become.

What are *you going to do about it?* he thought. The mirror, Zen-like, reflected back only his confusion.

Angus's cell phone rang, but for once he did not answer it.

Oh, I'm connected all right! PDA, cell phone, Internet, fax messages, 500 cable channels, the whole cyberspace nightmare! You would think if anybody had access to the answers it would be me. But I'm just like everybody else, walking around with a headset on, appearing to be mumbling to myself. It used to be if we were on the street talking to ourselves, we were considered crazy.

If only there were a delete button for dastardly days. Or maybe a do-over one. What was worse, this had been just a typical day for Angus. It had started with the alarm clock jack-hammering the billion neurons of his brain into consciousness. He had reached up in such a knee-jerk stupor that he knocked the clock off the table onto the hardwood floor, dividing it into two clocks, neither of them working. *Alarm.* That was the perfect start for Angus's day—frenzied —like fire ants in his boxers.

Had he set the alarm for an hour earlier, he would still have sabotaged himself. Some people travel in the fast lane, some are stuck in the slow lane. Angus was stuck in the *late* lane. Even when he planned extra time, he would squander it away in the shower in a hypothetical debate, bullying one of his colleagues into accepting one of his ideas, until the hot water ran out. Then he would notice the time, and the panic would begin anew.

Angus had rushed through the kitchen and kissed his daughter with the early morning pleasantry, "Sierra, I'm going to make it to your soccer game this afternoon." He went to kiss his wife, Carly, but his cell phone rang, so he answered it instead.

"Hello? Yeah, hello, Robert. Oh yeah? I figured that would happen. I'm surrounded by idiots, that's what I think of it."

Grabbing his coffee mug, he had rushed out the door with an affirmative grunt to his wife's query, "Coffee for breakfast again?" Carly could only sigh, looking down at the eggs she was about to scramble and then helplessly at her daughter.

"Sierra, he's just really busy these days. He's got big challenges at work. Don't be disappointed if he misses another game." She managed a smile for her daughter, and then quickly looked back at her eggs, disguising her own frustration.

3

But of course, Angus had missed the importance of that moment. He was deeply lost in the oblivion of the preoccupied, roaring down the highway, talking in his annoyed business voice to Robert on his cell phone, jacked up on coffee and anxieties, acting like an NFL linebacker blitzing on third down.

"All right, Robert. We've got problems. I'll be there soon."

He slammed the cell phone shut.

"Don't! Don't you dare!" he screamed at the traffic light turning red. *The longest red light in the city, and I have to get it.*

He had taken another gulp of his java while simultaneously flicking on the radio and dialing his office assistant on his cell phone. Angus could multitask with the best of them, a skill essential to the chronically late.

"Hi, Kelly. If Sterner gets in for our meeting before I do, tell him I'm on my way. I'm stuck in a major traffic jam!" A lie, of course, but not from his perspective. Everything was *always* major.

"What's that, Kelly? What does Harold want? A meeting tomorrow? Okay, okay, tell him I'll be there. See if you can free up my schedule."

Harold was his boss.

That's when Angus had started to sweat. He loosened his tie and unbuttoned his collar. *Isn't this red light ever going to change?* He could feel his heart pounding. Then he did that thing he always did under stress. He escalated. He took one worry (*Why does the boss want to see me?*) and created a catastrophic scenario around it (*I'm over budget, I'm not meeting deadlines, I'll get fired, Carly and Sierra will disown me, I'm going to die*). He had perfected this apocalyptic spiral of despair: he was a world-class down-hiller on a slippery slope.

Angus had been eyeing Eddy, the homeless guy who worked the red-light traffic for loose change. This had always irritated Angus and today it downright killed him. He wanted to yell, "Hey, Eddy, how about lending *me* a buck? You're even, and I'm down $18,000 in credit card debt!" But the light turned green, so Angus jumped on the horn instead.

The guy in the red truck in front of him made the obligatory gesture, which caused Angus, with a maniacal gleam, to accelerate around him, barely making the right-hand turn onto the freeway. He screeched to a halt behind the slow line queuing up for the freeway entrance. He had saved no time whatsoever, but to him, he had just sacked the quarterback.

But then came the guilt, the remorse, the worry: *Somebody could have gotten hurt and it would have been my fault.* Anger one minute, guilt the next.

He eventually wheeled into the packed company parking lot, smoldering as he looked for a space. He noticed one up front near his building, as well as a car approaching from the opposite direction with its blinker on. Another quick acceleration and Angus casually swerved into the space before the car could make the turn. It was rude, he knew, so he feigned innocence, although in the rear-view mirror he recognized the driver as an elderly woman who worked in his building.

At least it's not a fellow employee. I'm late and I need the space. This is an emergency.

He grabbed his briefcase and ran to the building.

"Mornin', Angus," came the happy, singsong voice of Daisy, the groundskeeper, who had been watering some small fir trees.

5

Some days that woman annoys me. Actually, most days. Doesn't she ever have a bad day?

He gave her a professional nod of recognition.

There is just no graceful landing possible from a horizontal position three feet off the ground. The garden hose that tripped him, combined with the speed at which he was moving, launched him skyward like a wounded condor, arms and briefcase flapping for balance. And losing. Prone on the sidewalk and cursing, Angus gathered himself up and hobbled into the building before Daisy, a big, lovable woman capable of carrying the perplexed Angus easily over one shoulder, could get there to help.

"Whoa! That was some flight, Angus! Are you still in one piece?"

Without looking back, Angus waved her off. *Can this day get any worse?*

It did. But there is no need to describe the rest of the misery that Angus created. More pulse-racing battles with time, anxiety rushes, and ego-related tailspins, real and imagined.

Angus had hoped that he could relax at home that evening, but all he saw were rush-hour stand-stills, a hundred e-mails, a disappointed daughter whose soccer game he had missed, and a detached wife who had had about enough of his unavailability.

And that was when his daughter had said, "The answers are always there, Daddy. You just have to look for them."

Angus found in the mirror the worry wrinkle that Sierra had pointed out. He traced it with his finger as if to erase it, but it did not go away. In this moment, for the first time, Angus recognized the truth of his situation.

❧

The Lift

Angus had a fitful night to match his day, this time fretting over his upcoming meeting with Harold, his boss. His conversation with his colleague Robert that morning confirmed a rumor he'd heard that his job as project manager for the new marketing plan was being questioned. Not just by his team, but by his boss. He had obsessed until he dozed off at 4:10 A.M., only to be jarred to attention by his daughter's alarm clock, which he had borrowed to replace the one he had broken the previous morning. The Disney tune was on full volume: "Zippity-do-dah, zippity ay."

No, this is not a "wonderful day"!

Fumbling unsuccessfully for the switch, he yanked the plug.

Angus rubbed his eyes and felt his tired body. He staggered to the shower and was drenched by a torrential downpour of warm water and cold thoughts. He stood aimlessly in the shower for who knows how long. It occurred to him that he was staring at his conditioner in his left hand, and couldn't remember whether he had shampooed or not. In his next fleeting glimpse of consciousness, he caught himself staring into the mirror holding his toothbrush but un-

7

clear as to whether or not he had brushed his teeth. Only the mint taste in his mouth gave him some confidence.

The next moment of awareness came while driving down his street. *Did I even see Carly and Sierra this morning?* The full coffee mug in his hand was an indicator that there had been an exchange, but the specifics were hazy.

If it is true that the world exists only in the present moment, then Angus's morning, full of ruminations about his upcoming meeting with his boss, had been nonexistent for all but an occasional blip on his screen of consciousness, usually associated with a gulp of caffeine.

The physical jolt of the car hitting the curb grabbed Angus's attention, causing him to grip the steering wheel tightly with both hands while grasping the thought that *yes,* he *was* driving by Hanford Park at 7:32 A.M., bumping along on a flat tire.

"No! No! Not today!" Angus raged as he pulled over alongside Hanford Park. He leaped out and saw the right back tire had been destroyed. Checking his watch and perspiring profusely, he opened the trunk and took out the jack. He got the lug nuts off and the car jacked up and went to grab the spare tire. He gave it a hopeful test bounce, but it replied with a splat.

Angus sank despondently to the curb, his determination and energy as flat as the spare tire he was staring at.

He pulled out his cell phone. "Kelly, it's me. Middle of rush-hour traffic and I'm sitting on the curb with a lug wrench in my hands, a flat tire, and a flatter spare. I'm a mess. If I look as crazed as I feel, I'd be arrested."

"I'm sorry, Angus," she replied kindly, and added, "But there is no hurry because Robert left a message saying he can't meet with you this morning."

Robert! Messing me up again!

Swelling with irritation, Angus jerked at his tie to loosen it.

"Why don't you take a little time, Angus?" Kelly, his long-time assistant, was trying to be helpful. "It sounds like you need it. You want to be calm and clear for your meeting with Harold this afternoon. You know how important it is."

"I know what I'm doing," snapped Angus, and hung up. *I'm fuming, that's what I'm doing.*

"You need a ride, sonny?"

He was startled by such a soothing sound; a breath of calm amid the rush-hour traffic. He turned in the direction of the voice. The first thing he noticed was the shoes—black, high-top Converse All Star basketball shoes, vintage early sixties. Then the gray sweat pants, classic old school with the baggy bottoms. Silver hair sprung out both sides of the man's head under his baseball cap. With a fatherly smile and twinkling eyes the old man stood with both feet firmly planted and his hands on his hips, a hybrid of Albert Einstein and Vince Lombardi. He could have been forty or ninety: his dynamic physical presence spoke of youth, but his deep wrinkles could only have been carved by decades of laughing smiles and arduous miles. Hypnotized by the stunning sight, Angus tilted his head.

"Maybe I need to ask in another language?" the old man laughed.

"Oh, no. It's just that, that, oh forget it," Angus stammered. "Yes, I would appreciate a lift. I just need to make a phone call first."

"Take your time."

Angus tossed his spare tire and tools back into the trunk, and called his service station on his cell. He scribbled a note, "Car repair truck on the way," and placed it under the wiper.

That's when Angus's memory kicked in.

"Hey," he said to the old man. "Aren't you the guy I see doing those strange-looking movements in the park every morning?"

"Strange to you, maybe," the old man laughed. "But very familiar to me. Something I learned from an old martial arts master, when I was the one who was needing a lift."

The old man bounded into a baby blue, '57 Chevy convertible in mint condition. Angus opened the car door and sat down. He blinked to clear his focus, and then looked at this strange being in the vintage hot-rod with a yin-yang symbol on the gearshift knob, a pair of fuzzy dice hanging from the rearview mirror, and immaculate white leather upholstery.

"I'm Angus. Thanks for the lift." His eyes toured the interior again. "This is some car."

"It's a good ride," replied the old man. And then he said, looking at Angus with piercing blue eyes, "Are you clear about where you desire to go?"

If it had been a normal "where would you like to go" Angus's response would have been immediate. He knew where the office was. He thought he knew where he was. Yet the old man's choice of words, and the way he said "clear," and "you," and "desire" gave direction-finding an entirely new meaning.

"Someplace different from where I seem to be headed," Angus sighed. Then he recovered with the more concrete, "I work at the Jefferson Building on Fourth and Federal."

"Well then, let's begin our journey. First, you need to fasten your centering belt."

"My what?"

"Oh! I know you call it a seat belt. But for me it's far more important than that."

"Centering belt?" Angus asked, bewildered.

"Wise words," the old man asserted.

"Weird words. The wisdom loses me." But Angus realized that nothing in his life was making any sense these days, so why not continue down this strange road?

"Do you have ten minutes before we proceed?"

"Not really," snapped Angus. "I'm a very busy man." *Who does this guy think he is? Time is money. God, I hate not being in control, stuck, dependent on this old geezer who probably wants to sell me something useless.*

He watched the old man start up the engine without hesitation or argument, his peaceful demeanor unchanged.

Okay, okay. My morning meeting has been canceled. And, well, maybe Kelly is right. I do need to pull myself together.

"On second thought, why not?" Angus responded, annoyed at the situation. "I've got a few extra minutes."

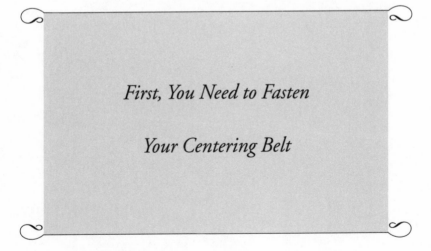

First, You Need to Fasten

Your Centering Belt

The First Breath

Hanford Park was unusually empty on this crisp fall morning. They left the car and Angus followed the old man to a little opening among some aspen trees, adjacent to a pond where ducks happily paddled about before they headed south for the winter.

"I am a small, elderly man, wouldn't you say?"

Before Angus could answer, the old man continued, "And you're a big strong guy. I want you to lift me up off the ground."

Now what have I gotten into? worried Angus, checking around anxiously to see if there were any observers.

"Use your legs so you don't hurt yourself and lift me up."

Angus glanced at his watch. *What possessed me to listen to this guy?*

Angus was a good six inches taller and seventy pounds heavier than the old man. He put his hands under the old man's arms and easily lifted him a foot off the ground.

"Thank you. Now place me back down."

Angus did as he was instructed, wondering about the sanity of the little man.

"I was right. You're very strong! Now I'm not going to

change anything physically, and I don't want you to change how you lift. Simply pick me up again."

Annoyed, Angus repeated his procedures. This time, to his amazement, he couldn't budge the old man. It was like trying to pick up the front of the old Chevy. Or pulling up one of the aspen trees. It would have been ludicrous to continue trying. This little man had suddenly become like a mountain.

Flustered and challenged, Angus's competitive instinct took over.

"I wasn't focused," asserted Angus. "Let me try that again."

Angus lifted. Nothing moved.

After a third try, Angus felt his frustration change to curiosity. He nervously looked around the park to make sure he was anchored to reality.

"What happened?" Angus was confused.

"I got centered," the old man said, as if it were a natural thing.

"I don't know what that is, but you felt twice as heavy."

The old man laughed. "Did you see me pour a slab of concrete down my pants? Centering is not about weight. It's about relationship. If I am separate from this earth, I'm easily lifted off of it. If I am connected to it, ah, then it is the whole earth you have to move."

Angus wondered who had dropped the hallucinogens in his coffee that morning.

"Now, stand with your feet about shoulder width apart. Look straight ahead." The old man lightly placed his hand on Angus's chest, and gently pushed. Angus wobbled backwards.

"This is how people are most of the time. Wobbly, at the

effect of every little pressure, every little stress, with no center. Right now, you have no center."

"How do I get one?" asked Angus, his cynicism melting into sincerity.

"It's a journey," the old man responded. "It starts in a very natural place: with your breathing."

"My breathing?"

"Yes. See if you can relax and simply notice your breathing. Put your hands on your belly. Now watch and feel this area. You will notice it is vitally alive! In your natural state you will be breathing deeply from this area. On inhalation your belly will expand outwards. On exhalation the belly will recede toward the spine."

Angus focused on his belly. Yes, it seemed to be moving. But his mind kept thinking about it rather than feeling it.

"I'm not sure I'm getting it."

"This is a common difficulty. Most people breathe shallowly from the chest. Simply notice the process without trying to do anything. It's like watching the ebb and flow of gentle waves on a beach. Try breathing through your nose. It will slow and deepen your breath. It might also help if you listen and follow the internal sound made as you breathe."

After a few breaths, Angus began to relax and pay full attention to his breath without hurrying.

"I think I'm getting it. But I'm not sure what 'it' is."

Angus couldn't imagine that simply breathing this way could be so fulfilling. However, he was aware that he rarely breathed this way, deep and full.

The old man smiled.

"That is the beginning of your Centering Breath. When you do deep, centered breathing, breathing with awareness, you will bring vital oxygen to every part of your lungs, particularly the lower lobes of the lungs where the oxygen-to-blood transfer is most efficient. You bring balance and health to your entire nervous system. Continue for another minute or so, with full attention to this Centering Breath."

After a few moments, Angus became acutely aware of his surroundings.

"Have those ducks been quacking since we got here?"

The old man smiled. "I can see by that question that you're understanding more about this Centering Breath. It's not just physical, not just relaxing and balancing the body. It's also mental, bringing you greater awareness and mindfulness. You are becoming more present.

"Look at those aspen trees. Listen to the ducks. Feel this gentle breeze. Nature is presenting you the gift of its beauty. Breathe all of this in—the oxygen and the experience—all the way to your center."

As he was saying this, he was lightly applying more pressure to Angus's chest, but this time, Angus was balanced.

"This is the amount of pressure that made you wobble the first time."

"No way!" Angus felt like a mountain. "I hardly feel any pressure now! Why? What am I doing?"

"You are becoming centered!" The old man let out another hearty laugh. "You don't feel the pressure when you are centered. Now take whatever it is you were doing or experiencing—a feeling, an image, a sound—and capture it. Increase it. If it's a picture, have it become more colorful and vivid. If it's a feeling, deepen it. If it's a sound, let it resonate at a higher quality. Simply intend, consciously choose, a more centered state."

Angus clearly felt more stable than he had for some time, but his doubt overruled him. *It can't be this easy, can it?*

"When you are ready, indicate with your hand and I will apply more pressure. I will apply it only gradually."

Tentatively at first, Angus began to wave in more pressure. Within seconds the old man announced, "Now I'm giving you twice as much pressure. Now it's three times. Now at least five times!"

Angus was not aware of the increase in pressure. He was too absorbed by the state of calm and presence that he felt. Moreover, he recognized that this feeling was not entirely new. It had occurred many times, in the simplest of moments, throughout his life. Simple images flooded back: he was a young child running through the shallow waves at the beach, or a young adult lying in a sleeping bag watching the Earth turn through the infinite starry canopy above. In those moments of mindfulness, as in this one, his analytical racing mind was less in the forefront of his consciousness, leaving his awareness clearer so the world could appear in the present moment, as it really is, fresh and vibrant. He was captivated by the revelation that he was an integral part of the world, not separate from it.

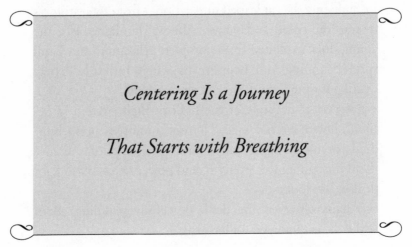

Centering Is a Journey

That Starts with Breathing

Finally, Angus said softly, "This is hard to believe. And all I'm doing is breathing deeply with awareness and looking at ducks."

The old man laughed again. His laughter didn't come superficially. It came from somewhere deep, an open-hearted, open-minded laugh, and the ducks and the aspen trees seemed to laugh with him. For the first time in a long time Angus felt relaxed and calm. The deep, full, deliberate breathing was surprisingly enjoyable.

After a while, the old man continued.

"Watch that cat sneaking up on that duck over there."

Angus looked toward the pond, where a large cat was crouched twenty yards away from the duck resting in the grass.

"The duck and the cat, like all of us, are blessed with autonomic nervous systems, involuntary systems that keep the heart beating, the lungs breathing, the stomach digesting. The autonomic nervous system is made up of two complementary systems. One is the 'fight-or-flight' system and the other is the 'rest-and-digest' system."

Suddenly the cat leaped into action—from total stillness to startling speed and power. Almost simultaneously, the young duck exploded from complete relaxation into a full sprint, running and flapping its wings furiously, barely making it to the pond, short a few feathers.

"A perfect example of the fight-or-flight system in action!" noted the old man. "It took hundreds upon hundreds of biochemical and neurological reactions to give them the endurance, strength, and power necessary to fight or flee. But look now."

Angus observed the duck peacefully paddling about while the cat lounged under a tree.

"Now, the rest-and-digest system is turned on to rebuild and rejuvenate. When one nervous system is turned on, the other starts shutting down. Full recovery is possible."

Angus nodded toward the road where they had met earlier and snarled, "It's just the opposite with the madness over there."

They watched the commuters in rush-hour traffic.

"You're right, Angus. Some are late for work or consumed by negative thoughts and worries. They get fixated on some fear or imagined catastrophe, and at least metaphorically they think that their lives are at risk. They speak to their bodies in dire language like 'I'm finished' or 'it's all over' or worse. The part of the human brain that is the headquarters of the autonomic nervous system has not evolved enough to make a distinction between death by saber tooth tiger and death by imaginary thoughts. So on goes the red alert switch—the fight-or-flight syndrome. Perspiration flows, eyes dilate, the sphincter and anus lock (which is a good thing!), the heart starts beating fast and hormones flood into the bloodstream preparing for the fight or flight. And the commuters just sit there! Hey! It's useless to leap out of your car and bite the fender of the truck in front of you. And yet that is what the fight-or-flight nervous system is preparing you to do."

"Is that why I get neurotic and a whole bunch of red flags on my blood test, while the animals over there by the pond don't? Because I don't get to burn off the chemicals in the fight or the flight?" Angus asked.

"That's only part of the answer. Let's say that despite all your rush-hour negative thoughts and distress, a miracle happens. When you get to your workplace, you find that everything is okay. You sit down at your desk and technically you could relax. The rest-and-digest system would get turned on, and it would rebuild and restore all of those chemicals released into the system. But the problem is that you don't relax, do you?"

"Heck, no. I'm only in the office for a few minutes before I get some call from a major client canceling her contract."

"Red alert!" smiled the old man.

"And then, just when you reconcile that, you get a memo from headquarters saying there is a company-wide layoff ahead."

"Red alert!" chuckled the old man. "And maybe you get through all of that mess successfully and can go home to relax. But you find yourself right back in rush-hour traffic. Red alert."

"Yeah, and then I finally make it home and there's spam in my mailbox, my daughter's sound asleep, and my wife has a headache! Red alert! Red alert! Red alert!"

"You got it. So what's the real problem? It's not the stress. Stress just is. Stress occurs when a significant change happens—mentally, physically, environmentally. It's part of our daily life—a river of change. The problem is that people today lack balance between the fight-or-flight system and the rest-and-digest system. We are on red alert far too much of the time."

"That's where centering comes in," the old man continued, with riveting intensity. "The autonomic nervous system is, for the most part, involuntary, meaning that it operates without your conscious involvement. For instance, it is difficult to consciously lower your blood pressure or immediately control your perspiration. But breathing is both involuntary and voluntary. Therefore, choosing deep centered breathing is one of the most powerful ways in which everyone can consciously and easily affect the autonomic nervous system. This centering provides you with a conscious choice. Deep centered breathing enables you to respond appropriately and mindfully, rather than react in a knee-jerk fight-or-flight manner when life doesn't go the way you want it to. Whenever you use this Centering Breath you bring balance and healing back.

"Now let's get you back to work."

Work! Angus marveled at the thought.

"This is the first time work hasn't preoccupied my mind and made me crazy since I woke up this morning," he said.

The old man put a hand on his shoulder and looked at him with compassion. "*Work* doesn't make you crazy. You choose that state."

Centering Does Not Take Time—

It Takes Intention

Centering

The old man could have been Angus's grandfather, yet he moved smoothly, catlike.

Angus climbed into the passenger seat of the Chevy. "This is fascinating, this centering thing," he said. "But the truth is that I have no time to practice it." He had already begun to worry about work and his busy life.

"Centering does not take time—it takes intention," responded the old man. "In fact, when you are calm and more present, you will save time. You don't need time to be happy."

"Maybe I'll do it during lunch break," replied Angus.

"Great, but why not right now?" the old man suggested. "You could start by fastening your—"

"My centering belt?" Angus interrupted with a grin.

"That's right," chuckled the old man. "That belt, even that click you hear when you fasten it, can be a wake-up call to get centered. You don't have to wait till 'later.' And notice, the belt fits right over your centering area."

Angus hooked up the seat belt and, in spite of himself, he found himself taking some deep centering breaths.

"I feel 'centered' right now, I think," Angus observed.

"But, I'm not sure I have the discipline to remind myself to do it."

They pulled up to a red light. The old man smiled.

"If you added up all the time you've spent at red lights, how long do you think that would be?"

"That's a frightening thought."

"It certainly is! Wanting to go while you're being forced to stop can be stressful. But only if you believe that the time spent is wasted, making you late or anxious or conflicted. But what if you think of those red-light moments, which might add up to weeks or months over a lifetime, not as wasted time but as opportunities to get centered—more aware, more healthy, more connected than ever before."

"Sounds better than watching my blood pressure go up."

The old man nodded.

"So here is our first—not 'red light'—but 'centering light'! We now have time to take a Centering Breath!"

Angus took a deep breath through his nose. He felt his body naturally aligning. He sat up straight to become more symmetrical, placing his head directly upon his spine, with his arms and legs relaxed. As he breathed, he had the feeling that his head was being suspended from the top, as if his vertebrae were a string of beads being stretched, one suspended lightly above the other. His hands rested easily on his lap.

The light changed to green.

"All right, I was just starting to get into that centered feeling. My body feels suspended. Time feels suspended. It feels good."

Angus could feel his cynicism disappearing breath by breath, which—given his years of practicing it—felt unusual.

"Now you want longer red lights!" the old man wise-cracked.

Within minutes they found themselves at another red light.

"Finally!" the old man faked exhaustion. "Here is another centering opportunity. Now besides aligning the body, let's focus on another aspect of the Centering Breath. Focus on bringing in energy and releasing tension. On the inhalation, see and feel all the energy you need entering your body. Let it settle deep into your center and radiate it to every cell in your body. On the exhalation, let go of tension. Visualize a waterfall running freely through the body, releasing any tension."

Angus took several deep Centering Breaths. He was energized and relaxed at the same time.

"Excellent," the old man smiled. "Keep exploring that until the next red light."

A minute later they were there.

"Another aspect of this Centering Breath is to observe the present moment. Breathe in this present moment—the sounds, the colors, the textures, the feelings. On the exhalation, see the thin veil of separation between you and your environment dissolve. Flood the environment with your good energy; increase your connection to this moment. Take a deep breath and tell me what you notice."

Angus looked around with as much awareness as he could muster. He saw a sweet-faced woman walking a quick-stepping cocker spaniel. A porch decorated with pumpkins, colorful gourds, and dried corncobs. The fascinating patterns of the city skyline against the crisp blue sky.

"I've driven this street hundreds of times," said Angus, "but I'm seeing it so differently now. Where have I been?"

"Where most people are—trapped in the worry of past and future. And all the while the universe dances its beautiful dance unnoticed."

A man in a large SUV turned abruptly into their lane, causing the old man to slam on his brakes to avoid a collision.

Angus exploded simultaneously, "What a jerk! Talk about a total lack of awareness! I'd like to get a hold of that yahoo and hold him down while you slap him a dose of this centering stuff!"

"Sounds like you really have this work down," the old man chuckled, looking at Angus closely to make sure he was kidding.

He wasn't. Angus was hot. "Yeah? Well, I'd love to knock that turkey out of my 'present moment' and into next week!"

"Sounds like you're in last week and not in the present moment, Angus. What makes you so convinced he's a bad guy?"

"Hey. We could have been injured back there."

"That was a 'could have' that didn't happen."

There was a moment of silence before the old man continued.

"What if we were to track down that guy and find out that he's rushing to the hospital because his wife is in heavy labor, or his father is having a stroke?"

"Well, then I guess he's just unconscious."

"But is he a bad person with the malicious intent to hurt us?"

"No."

"Haven't we all done some stupid things in our lives, especially under stress?"

"Yeah, I guess." Angus began to consider his present predicament. "Many, in my case."

The old man looked at Angus's chagrin with a grandfatherly mixture of love and wisdom.

"Compassion and kindness aren't just for a saintly few. They are works of art that we all can develop as we become more centered and present."

"You're right," Angus observed, realizing with reluctance that this was going to be a long journey. "As you can tell, I can't control my emotional outbursts, especially when I see things that I think are wrong."

"Well, you actually *can* control your outbursts. You begin by taking a deep Centering Breath just before you react. Didn't your parents give you the ancient kitchen wisdom, 'count to ten' before acting?"

"Sure," Angus laughed, "but the problem was they never did it themselves."

The old man bounced with laughter in his white leather seat.

"Look at the sky and tell me what the weather is."

"Clouds are rolling in."

"But it was clear only minutes ago! Wait another hour and it could be snowing. Emotions are just like that. They are simply an internal weather pattern. Like the weather outside, they are always changing. We can feel and learn from our emotions without getting plugged into them. Centering allows us to be present with them. And we always have a choice. We can decide to enjoy a walk, even though the sun's not out."

It bugs me the way this old geezer keeps making sense. But darn it—he's right. The problem is, how will I remember to do it?

They drove on. The old man glanced at a large billboard on his right:

BIG T TIRES
FREE BALANCING AND ALIGNMENT
DO IT TODAY!

"What does that sign say to you, Angus?"

"It says somebody wants my money. They must have seen me sitting on the curb with two lousy tires."

"Now, read it out loud, just the second line and the last line."

" 'Free balancing and alignment, do it today.' "

Angus recentered, confirming that he got the point.

"One gazillion megabytes of information are thrown at us every moment. We can't possibly take it all in. We get to choose what we want to take in. That sign can be not just an advertisement, but another valuable centering cue, like the red light. If we are open, the support is everywhere we look. It's always our choice."

The old man pulled to a stop in front of Angus's office building. Angus got out of the car and turned to him, mesmerized by this strange man with those black high tops, sitting in that baby blue Chevy with that yin-yang gearshift. He shook his head in amazement.

"I don't know how to thank you. All this on the way to work! I'm going to go write down what you've taught me."

"Writing it down would be good, but beware. Most people write things down and just put them away. They trivialize the work this way. They don't realize that there is a distinction between information about centering and the actual mind/body practice of centering.

"Information is horizontal; a mind/body art is vertical,

diving ever deeper. Information just gets stashed away some-place, in a computer or book. But a mind/body discipline gets practiced, explored, and developed daily. Great artists, athletes, entrepreneurs, and even 'enlightened people' be-come that way not by happenstance, but by practicing day after day. The great artist Monet painted the same field of flowers for over thirty years because they were never the *same*. Each day they were alive, anew, with unique mean-ing."

Angus agreed, "I bet Einstein never awoke saying 'Darn! I've got to get up and spend all day doing that relativity thing again!'"

"That's right!" the old man exclaimed. "He chose it! It was what his life was about. And great athletes play their sport for the joy of it. They would still do it if they received no money, and no one was watching. It is the daily practice of centering that will nurture the seed of awareness and presence to grow, allowing your full authentic self to blos-som, and put a fire in your belly. My advice is simple. Keep doing centered breathing. Create as many cues as you can, like the red lights, billboards, anything to remind you to practice."

"Or cell phone rings?" Angus began to consider the myriad of reminders that he could use—the shower, wait-ing for the computer to boot up, even the alarm clock!

"Yes!" The old man locked his attention on Angus. "Let's do it now. One deep centered breath. On the inhala-tion, take in balance and energy. On the exhalation, release all tension while connecting fully to the present moment."

Angus and the old man took one deep breath together. Angus couldn't remember ever feeling this alive.

"When you take a deep Centering Breath you will begin

to calm the two great storms which cause your suffering. One is the storm of your mind and the other is the turbulence of your body. Deep centered breathing can calm them both. When the storms subside, the spirit soars."

"This has been an extraordinary morning of learning," said Angus, looking gratefully at the old man.

"It's an exciting journey!"

"What comes next?" Angus asked anxiously.

"The learnings are right in front of you. Everywhere you look is your master teacher in disguise."

The old man quickly waved good-bye and pulled away from the curb.

"Wait!" shouted Angus. He didn't even know the old man's name!

Angus stood on the curb and wrote in his PDA:

The Centering Breath
Breathe in the present moment,
with balance and energy

The Centering Breath

Breathe in the present moment,

with balance and energy

A Master Teacher in Disguise

Angus settled into his office. His unfamiliar sense of light-ness and ease was soon fogged by concern over his meeting regarding his project team, of which he was head. He real-ized that he needed to reestablish his credibility when he met with Harold today. His performance and his attitude were being scrutinized. And today he could understand why. He recognized an unproductive pattern in himself. He often *was* uncentered, full of anger and blaming. The truth was that he *did* doubt himself. And the more he doubted, the more he had to justify.

His thoughts returned to the morning's strange events. What if he tried the "centering" that the old man had showed him? Maybe it could help him relax a little. He set-tled into his chair and closed his eyes. At first it felt a little contrived and analytical. But after several breaths, he felt his anxiety relaxing. After a few more breaths Angus no-ticed that he was able to detach himself from his analysis and simply witness his thought process. There were "the thoughts," and then there was "the person who was think-ing those thoughts," the observer, who could simply watch without getting attached or reactive. Angus realized that, rather than getting plugged in to his thoughts, he could be watching a play, one in which he was the director and actor at the same time. If he wanted to, he could cut and do a retake, choosing an entirely different role for himself.

He realized that he actually had a choice.

The truth was, Angus didn't like the unavailable and argumentative character that he had been playing lately. What kind of character could he choose to take its place? Did he have the power and courage to let that new character show up?

I've got to get my energy and joy back. If I don't, I have no business on this stage playing the role of team leader.

Uncertain how to proceed, Angus tried another deep Centering Breath. He felt present, as he had with the old man. In his silence, he heard a faint song coming from outside. The more he listened, the more relaxed he became. The song was coming from Daisy, the company groundskeeper, raking leaves below his window, singing out with freedom and feeling.

Something about that singing made him realize: *That woman is centered.* He had been piling up excuses brick by brick, imprisoning himself. And there was Daisy, on the lowest end of the corporate hierarchy, singing out her happiness for all the world to hear.

If only I could be that free.

The old man's words echoed in his mind, "The learnings are right in front of you. Everywhere you look is your master teacher in disguise."

Without quite knowing why, Angus got up and went outside.

Angus realized that he had never really spent any time on the beautifully kept grounds around his office, nor had he attempted more than just a reluctant hello to Daisy, the person responsible for its beauty. As he walked over to where she was raking, he realized he had never before left the sidewalk and walked on the company grounds.

"I was just noticing how vibrant it feels out here, Daisy. You really do a magnificent job."

Daisy looked at her unlikely visitor.

"Thanks. Glad to see nothing is hurt after yesterday's heroic attempt at human flight."

Angus chuckled, recalling his uncentered stumble over the garden hose.

Returning her smile with one of his own, a rare sight indeed, he replied, "If I had just dropped my briefcase and worked on my arm flap, I'd have been airborne."

Both laughed out loud. Both! Angus was surprised at his joy and spontaneity. Yesterday, Daisy's cheerfulness had soured him, but today Angus was choosing to have a different experience. He saw her as the big lovable mother hen of the company grounds that she was. He noticed her strong calloused hands and sensed in her a wisdom about all things natural. He was comforted by the thought that, if ever the concrete jungle of modern city living came crashing down, here was someone who could teach others how to survive and flourish on the good, green Earth. He felt that the big red bandanna stuffed into her pocket could be used in a hundred ways, from picking up needled branches to wiping away tears.

"Comin' out to enjoy the last of these glorious fall days?" Daisy looked at the sky. "Snow's on the way, I know it."

"I heard you from my office window, singing like a bird," Angus said to her.

"You better listen to some real birds before you say that!"

They both paused to listen to the birdsong around them. It was like a light-hearted symphony, each bird carrying a different, delightful melody.

"That's singin'!" Daisy said with authority.

Angus stared into the flowing creek nearby. He wondered why some people seemed to have found their song, their ability to be happy, whereas others like himself hadn't found it, or if they had, had been too afraid to sing it out to the world. He desperately needed to find the answer. *Might this woman, Daisy, be a teacher in disguise?* He summoned his courage with a Centering Breath.

"Daisy, are you happy all the time?"

Daisy didn't answer right away, but instead she looked down at the ground. Angus thought he detected a feeling of pain in her face.

"You don't have to answer that," Angus back-pedaled, feeling he might have gone too far. "That's really none of my business."

"No," Daisy replied. "You asked it, so that makes it both our business."

"You just seem to have this song about you, this youthful essence that you radiate."

Still looking at the ground, she began to nod her head slowly.

"I do. Yes, I do, most days. Yes, I do."

The words spoke of agreement, but her solid shoulders seemed to stoop as she stood watching the stream.

"What is it, Daisy?" he asked. Angus realized with alarm that he was positioning himself in the unfamiliar role of listener.

Daisy worked hard for the right words.

"My Mama told me there's a song in everything. But if you don't sing it, it don't get heard."

"Did your mother teach you to sing?"

"Yes," she said. "She did. I would sing day and night. I'd sing about flowers, and clouds, and everything around me. I just made it up." She paused. "But then I stopped singin'."

"Tell me," said Angus softly. "What happened?"

Angus surprised himself with his own availability. *But don't I have a meeting to prepare for? What am I thinking, inviting this kind of conversation? On the other hand, could it be that I'm on the verge of a critical learning?*

That observation centered Angus. So, when Daisy took a seat on the rock by the stream, Angus sat down beside her.

"Years ago I lived with my Mama and Grandma. Mama had me when she was fifteen years old. She kept a tight leash on me, she did, cuz she did not want to see me doin' what she did so young like that. I sang in the choir and I learned to plant in the garden and take care of the neighbors' flowers and I even taught myself to build rock gardens outta the rubble in the old back lots."

"Did you build this beautiful garden here?" asked Angus.

"Yes, I did," was her reply. "And all those over there, too."

Angus looked at the beautiful rock gardens which surrounded him, just beginning to appreciate how Daisy had turned her life of work into a work of art.

"So, you had your song back then," observed Angus.

"Yes, I did," said Daisy, drawing in a deep breath. "But then, I got in with some bad kids and I started doin' things I should'na. And I liked this one boy."

She stopped speaking, and Angus knew in his mind what her next words would be.

"And, I had his baby."

He had guessed right.

"How old were you?"

"I was fifteen."

The stream flowed steadily through the well-placed rocks of the garden, bringing a sense of calm, of resolve, encountering obstacles and managing to keep on flowing.

"I thought that if I'd have his baby, I'd have him. But I was wrong. My Mama told me that, but I didn't believe her. But she was right."

Angus exhaled fully, "I'm sorry Daisy."

Daisy looked directly at Angus with a spark in her eyes, "But, I could still garden, sew, chop wood, and, well, I jus' knew how to survive."

"I'm sure you did."

"But Social Services didn't understand that." Daisy looked at the ground and shook her head.

"What do you mean?"

"Grandma was sick, so Mama couldn't work, and I couldn't work cuz of the baby. We had no runnin' water or electricity and just an outhouse in the back, so I guess they figured that might be—what do they call it?—substandard. Anyway, I heard from some friends that they might come and check on things, and maybe take the baby away." She turned her head again.

Angus wanted to blurt out, "They can't do that!" but he took another Centering Breath instead.

"I sat in my rockin' chair and cried like a baby and the baby cried right along with me. I thought about how I'd fight them like an old grizzly protecting her cub if they came. I cried. I cursed. I raged. And I must admit I didn't take good care of myself. I knew that any day Social Services would be knocking on my door to take my baby away. Finally, I was so spent, I just let go. And that's exactly when it came to me. 'Girl, what are you doing? Why yell and scream and fight and hurt yourself like that? That gonna tell them for sure this Mama's no good!' "

"What did you do?" asked Angus, entranced.

"It was late at night and I was real quiet. I began to see a picture in my mind—a picture of my best self—the 'me' that could sing my song, even if it had to start out as a little hum. I focused so much on this picture of a strong lovin' Mama who could raise a beautiful baby and a beautiful garden at the same time, that it came to me as natural as my breathin'. In fact, when I sat and rocked my baby, I'd breathe that picture into every cell in my body."

Breathing! thought Angus. *Could this be another breath, another deep learning, that the old man had hinted at?*

"So what happened with Social Services and the kids?" Angus asked anxiously.

"Well, they showed up after a few weeks," Daisy looked up with a Cheshire-cat grin. "My case worker's name was Megan and she must've seen something that made her look past the poverty and believe in me.

"Every week Megan would come to check on me, and every week she'd see a Mama who—instead of complaining or actin' hopeless or any of that—was singin' or smiling' or doin' her best. And when the summer came, Megan got to see the neighborhood come alive with all the flowers that I planted."

"They never had cause to take your baby!" asserted Angus.

"Not only that," added Daisy. "They got me this job right here!"

"Wow!" Angus acknowledged. "That's quite a story."

They both stared at the water in the stream as it made its gurgling way around the rocks. After a long centered moment, Angus knew he needed to learn more.

The Second Breath

"Could you tell me more about this breathing?" Angus asked Daisy. "What do you mean by breathing this strong loving 'Mama' in?"

Daisy turned her attention from the flowing stream to Angus.

"Well, I don't know what to tell you. All I know is that every day I breathe in the 'me I want to be' and Daisy here still keeps growin'! My daughter graduated high school and is now enrolled in City College. I guess anything is possible!"

Angus took a deep Centering Breath. *It was possible for Daisy to be the best 'me' she could be. She had turned that possibility into reality. It came from consciously breathing it in. Breathing! The second breath! The Possibility Breath! Breathe in the highest possible me!*

It sounded wonderful, but he was unclear as to how to do it.

"What do you mean, breathing it into every cell?" asked Angus. "Do you mean just really believe and hope that you're that person?"

"It's not just a strong belief or hope. That's just left up here." Daisy lightly touched her head. "When you breathe

41

it into your mind and body, you become it, you know it. Heck, you are it."

"Could you show me?" Angus was now an open-minded student.

"Maybe." Daisy paused, not knowing where to begin. She took in the sights and sounds around them. Then she got up and Angus followed her over to a stand of aspen trees. Nearby were piled some thick dead branches, one of which she took into her calloused hands.

"What's gonna happen if you put pressure on this branch?" She handed it to him.

"It will break."

He bent the dead branch, and it broke with a snap. Then she reached over to one of the live branches on the aspen tree.

"This live branch is about the same size. Do you think you could break this branch in two?"

"Let's see," replied Angus.

Angus put his hands on the healthy young branch. No sooner had he begun than he laughed out loud. "Daisy, you know this is silly. There is no way I can break this branch. It's alive, it's pliable. It's not like that rigid, dead one."

"I think there are different ways to try to be strong," said Daisy. "When I was angry and cursin' and ragin', that was one kind of strong. I was like that dead branch, kind of like this." Daisy stiffly held out her arm and immediately tightened her hand into a fist.

"Try to bend my arm, Angus."

"Oh, no, I can't. I don't want to do that."

"Just do it."

The conviction in her voice was enough. Angus put one hand on her upper arm and took her wrist with his other hand and gave sort of a half attempt to bend her arm at the elbow.

"Come on, really try," she said, then clenched her teeth and tightened even more.

Angus increased the pressure, quite a bit—for she was a strong woman—and then bent her arm in a sudden and jolting collapse.

"Did that hurt?"

"A little."

"I'm sorry."

"I asked for it. That's what happens when you're angry and stubborn. You're rigid, and when you break, you really break. Like that dead branch. There's no life in it. But there is a way to be strong that does work."

Daisy held her arm out again. "Now try to bend my arm."

Angus took her arm as before. It felt different this time, pliable, soft, and alive, like the living aspen branch. He tried to bend it, but he couldn't. Then he adjusted his hold, leaned into it, and tried again, but it was clear that the arm was just not going to fold. *How could this woman be so powerful?*

"Teach me that, Daisy," said Angus eagerly, sensing that, as with the old man, these learnings were taking place in both the mind and the body. He stood up and put his arm out straight in front of him.

Daisy let her hand brush easily over his arm from his shoulders to his fingers.

"It is no longer just an arm. It's a living branch. Or better yet, it's a flowin' river as powerful as you want to make it. Breathe in the very best of you, the 'me you want to be.' Take some deep breaths, and let it in."

Angus started to breathe deeply. He understood that

part from the old man. But what did she mean "the me I want to be"? The powerful "me" that he had always identified with was a tight-fisted bulldog fighting fiercely to win his way to success. And now he could see that that "me" was nothing but an old dead branch.

Daisy sensed his confusion.

"Do you have anyone, anything that you love beyond all doubt?" Daisy asked, eyes sparkling with energy.

"My daughter," came the immediate reply.

"Then picture her there, way out there, way past the trees that you are pointing to with your arm. The 'me' you want to be is the 'me' that feels a flow of love. Feel it flowin' like a big river, bathin' your daughter in that energy. Give that energy a color so that you can see the flow going from your whole self, through your arm, and out to her. Hear a continuous sound flowin' out to her along with that feeling and that color."

With a lump in his throat, Angus thought of Sierra. He saw her in her soccer uniform, dribbling the ball down the field, hair flowing, running free. He felt a stream of energy flowing from him to her, bathing her in love and protection. The strength of this bond was such that he felt more connected to her in that moment than he often had in her actual physical presence.

Daisy tried as hard as she could to bend his arm, but she couldn't do it.

"Yes, indeed! That's true power."

Angus, without question, could feel the effect of this exercise, not just on his arm, but also on his entire being.

He was no longer trying, clenching. Instead, he was just being. His experience of power and presence was extraordinary. Angus had the distinct feeling that it wasn't all about ego; that it wasn't "his" power operating. It was something mysterious, that he couldn't yet describe. He figured, as the old man had said, there was even more to learn.

"What a feeling," was all he could muster.

Daisy recognized the state he was in.

"You're finding your song, Angus!"

Angus stood mesmerized. He was astonished that he had *chosen* to participate in this flow of energy, now, in the moment. He could *choose* it at any time. He thought of the old man's words: "It doesn't take time, it takes intention."

"You seem to sing your song all day long," Angus found himself saying.

"I have a song that is always there, like what you have with your daughter. And that song shows up in whatever's on my plate that day. Like rakin' these leaves. But it's not about rakin' leaves; it is much bigger than that. It's what we put into it that makes the song come alive."

Daisy walked back to her rake.

Angus was so grateful that he had chosen to follow this simple, happy gardener around the company grounds and question her with the wide-eyed enthusiasm of a young child. He had hardly spoken to her in all the years they had seen one another. What a "disguise" this teacher came in!

"But don't you get up some days with no motivation or power to do it?"

"Sure I do! But that's just another story, another excuse to hold you back. That's when I breathe in real deep and just be the me I want to be. And that 'me' is one that doesn't let her stories, her excuses, hold her back. I mean, I always have a good story. Don't you?"

Angus nodded his head in agreement. He began to reflect on some of his own stories and how he used them to keep himself from choosing a state of joy and power. *I have to work day and night to earn a living—that's why I don't have time to go to Sierra's game. Nobody agrees with me on the project team—that's why we can't get the job done. Come to think of it, I have lots of stories. Maybe I could find my true power when I let my life flow without any stories to hold me back.*

"What do I do with all my stories?" he asked.

Daisy paused for a long moment.

"I'm not sure. What do you think?" was her honest reply.

"Maybe I should acknowledge them. Just feel and learn from them," said Angus. "Then they won't hold me back."

"That's what I think, too," said Daisy, sharing his discovery. "Just don't live out of them! Heck, it's cuz of the roughest winters and driest summers that I learned how to grow vegetables, harvest and store them right. I don't live out of my mistakes anymore—I learn from them, and then

True Power Is When You Have Life

Flowing Through You Without

Any Stories to Hold You Back

I just breathe in the me I want to be, the one that's bigger than my story. I breathe it into every cell and I sing it out to my world. And sometimes my world is rakin' leaves and sometimes it's talkin' to people like you who put down their cell phones long enough to listen to the music. So I'll just grab that rake, and put my body and soul into it. Heck, I put my whole song into it."

Angus looked into Daisy's wise eyes, and took a deep Centering Breath. "Thank you, Daisy," he said to her. "You've given me a very important learning, a new kind of breath I need everyday—a Possibility Breath. At any time I can breathe in power and purpose and the me I want to be."

Daisy smiled.

Angus felt like a little boy who had just learned how to whistle.

The Possibility Breath

⟲

Breathe in the "me I want to be"

with power and purpose

Possibility

Angus reentered his office with determination. He sat at his computer, recalled the day's learnings, and created a new screen saver for his computer:

The Centering Breath
*Breathe in the present moment,
with balance and energy*

The Possibility Breath
*Breathe in the "me I want to be"
with power and purpose*

Then he printed out a smaller copy—for the dashboard of his car.

One pinned to the inside of my brain would be nice, too, he thought.

Angus approached Harold's office. Previously, whenever Angus had gone to see Harold he had been nervous, the kind of nervous that comes when you see a police car in your rearview mirror—you haven't done anything wrong, yet you're expecting flashing lights.

As he walked down the corridor, he focused on Harold's door. The doorknob was going to be his new "centering cue," he decided. He took a Centering Breath, a deep inhale, aligning his posture and taking in awareness, and then a long exhale, releasing tension and being present. Then he took a Possibility Breath, accessing his highest level of self —the "me" he wanted to be, without all his stories and excuses. He filled every cell in his being with the essence of a true team player, ready to do his part one hundred percent and to be the leader that he knew he could be.

Angus turned the doorknob and entered.

"Harold, it's good to see you," he said, sincerely, and went up to shake hands with his boss.

Harold was an ex-military man in his mid-fifties. His strong, stocky build and his flattop spoke volumes for his toughness and discipline.

Harold stood up and gave Angus a handshake that could have crushed walnuts.

"You seem more at ease today, Angus," Harold observed.

"I am working on myself," said Angus calmly.

Angus sat down, once more aware of his own fears and concerns. He gratefully took another Centering Breath.

Angus had consciously chosen to see Harold in a new way today. He was aware that it was going to take everything he had recently learned to keep from reacting in his same old excusing, story-laden manner.

Having Harold as my boss makes me sweat, to say nothing of the man's physical presence, his past military medals, and his no-frills, no-b.s. talk!

Angus breathed in the possibility of seeing Harold as exactly the man he needed to help him be the best "me" he could be. Immediately Angus began to see specific positive aspects of the man sitting in front of him. *I can count on this man to tell me the truth. If I need to change he'll be there to let me know when I fall off the path. He has continually delegated and empowered his people. He has always backed his people with real support when they earned it. Having him as my boss is a great opportunity.*

As Angus focused on Harold's gifts, he felt centered and purposeful. The stern features on the face of the man in front of him seemed to soften. *Is this my perception or did that actually happen? Does the answer to that question even matter?*

"Angus, you're the head of a very important marketing project that must be rolled out by the end of the next quarter. It is critical to our success. As you know, it has to be done with impeccable quality, on time, and within budget. We are already a month into it, Angus, and I've got some concerns." Harold paused for a long moment, looking down at his hands. And then directly at Angus.

"How's it going, Angus?"

Angus's first instinct was to explain and defend himself, to blame Robert, to critique the others. Instead, Angus took a deep Possibility Breath and remembered the lesson with Daisy.

The desire to blame comes from my story, my litany of excuses. My story is something to feel and learn from but certainly not my highest purpose. It's not the "me I want to be."

In his newfound calmness, as truthfully as he could, he told Harold the present-moment reality.

"We are a couple of weeks behind in the planning process, we are ten percent over budget due to some design changes, and there are some internal personnel conflicts that need to be resolved if we are to operate as a high-performance team." Angus's body was aligned and balanced, his attention fully engaged with Harold, and his communication direct and congruent. He continued to breathe deeply.

Harold was surprised. He had expected Angus to sugar-coat his answer, complete with blame and excuses. This would have given Harold good reason to question whether Angus was cut out to be the project leader—and to consider removing him from that project. He simply nodded his head, put his huge forearms on his desk, and leaned forward.

"Tell me, Angus. Should I have confidence that you can do this job?"

"My team and I will do this job together, Harold. There are crucial changes that I now know need to be made—including many within myself. I have renewed faith that those changes will be made, that we can gain back the energy and presence to do whatever is purposeful for this project to be a massive success."

Harold nodded his head, impressed with Angus's congruity.

"Angus, you've got a lot to do. I look forward to a full report next week; same time, same place." Harold stood up and went over to Angus, put his hand on his shoulder, and led him to the door.

"Angus, I'm accountable for this company and therefore this project. It has not been working, and as head, I am counting on you. You showed me something powerful today and it only took a few minutes. I know changes need to happen with your team"—Harold locked his eyes on Angus—"and it starts with you. I still believe you can make it work. Don't hesitate to let me know how I can support you."

"Thank you, Harold," said Angus. As much as he struggled to admit it, he added, "You're right. And I've already begun to make some of those changes in myself."

Angus returned to his own desk, loosened his tie, and heaved a sigh of relief.

Man, did that go better than I expected, he thought, looking at the "Two Deep Breaths" on his screensaver.

None of the excessive explanations and justifications the way I usually do. The power of center cut right to the core of what Harold was looking for. And what I was looking for in myself.

Yet even though the meeting had gone well, there was still something nagging at Angus, something missing, something that made him uneasy. He didn't know what it was.

There is a lot of stress and conflict going on with the project team. There is something about my approach that not only fails to solve the difficulties, but actually exacerbates them.

Haven't I always been strong and forceful in leadership, and articulate in my communication? Why is it that my attempts fail so often? Aren't my ideas right? What am I doing wrong? Is there another "story" that's holding me back?

Even with his two breaths, the Centering Breath and the Possibility Breath, he feared that his ability to work with his team, or even his family for that matter, was still uncertain. There was something else he needed to learn.

The Third Breath

"Thanks for fixing the tires," Angus called out as he pulled out of his service station and headed for home. The surprise autumn snow had started to fall an hour before and it was coming down heavily now.

The mechanic watched him drive away. "I think that's the first time I've seen that guy without a frown. He actually talked to us!"

At the first centering light, Angus stared at the "Deep Breaths" card that he had taped to the dashboard. He took a deep Centering Breath. He felt a calmness surround him. Usually blizzard conditions like these would have made him tense and anxious. He let his awareness be open to "seeing" beyond his preoccupations. He just started observing the present moment, just as the old man had suggested. He was soon fascinated by the different shapes of the snowflakes as they hit the windshield. He noticed the patterns the wind made with the falling snow in the headlights. He listened to the sound of his tires driving through the snow, and the rhythm of the wipers.

At another stoplight, he glanced at himself in the rearview mirror. His attention went right to the "worry" wrinkle that Sierra had pointed out. Was it his imagination, or was his brow somewhat less furrowed than usual? He scanned his face and noticed that he naturally had a half-smile on his lips. It kind of took him by surprise. He deliberately frowned, and noticed how his eyes squinched together and the deep furrow returned. Then he breathed a deep breath, and smiled, and the furrow softened even more.

When I get "centered," my body relaxes and I literally open up, Angus noticed. *Even my face transforms.*

His half-smile grew a little when he passed the tire sale sign that the old man had pointed out that morning. The word "Alignment" again stood out. Angus looked again at the Deep Breaths card he had taped on his dashboard and focused on the second breath, the Possibility Breath. An image of an aligned team flooded his consciousness: a joyful, talented, committed team. No frowns!

No way that's happening with my team, Angus argued with himself. *Our project is more like a battleground of fighting egos than a team.*

Haven't I been excruciatingly clear about what should happen? Haven't all my wise ideas and solutions been met with resistance, no matter how hard I have worked on persuading the team otherwise? Wasn't that the way it worked in any group—hammer at each other until someone emerged triumphant?

Angus relived the endless, nauseating meetings and his collisions with Robert.

"So," Angus would begin, "Here's what I would like to propose . . ."

And a few sentences into it, Robert would pipe up.

"But, Angus, that will never work because ..."

Within minutes, the energy of the idea would be deflated into a series of debates about why it couldn't work.

That's when Angus realized something crucial. *I haven't been helping the situation. I've been setting up Robert as my adversary. I'd make my proposal, and Robert would counter it. But what did I do then? I'd seek my revenge: I'd manage a way to make him wrong—and his half-baked schemes, too.*

Painfully Angus became aware of how he and Robert had set a precedent of a "me or you" attitude that had infiltrated the entire team, until no one was willing to be creative and supportive anymore. Angus and Robert had modeled and built a high-powered "yes, but" gang of individuals who could effectively kill any good idea. It was always a fight to be right.

When he approached the entrance to the highway, a road sign grabbed his attention. He let up on the gas at the YIELD sign, letting the other vehicles in. He realized he had never stopped to appreciate the sign's hidden lesson. It was so obvious that it was almost trite.

Yield? Now there was a concept he had rarely considered, except as a traffic necessity. *Yield to other vehicles, of course. If you don't, you will have an accident. But yielding to others in the workplace or at home?* He studied the sign.

Maybe I don't let anyone in, he realized.

How many collisions have I gotten into with people because I didn't yield? I always figured someone else was trying to be right, which meant I'd have to admit I was wrong. No way was I going to do that! But what about "yielding" to listen to another's opinion, ideas, the need to contribute, with the actual possibility that I might be wrong? If a highway can handle all the vehicles, maybe our team, starting with me, can learn to honor one another's input. We need to change the "yes, but" dogfight into a "yes, and" team.

So ... how can I make that happen?

Angus thought about the different personalities on his team. They all had different strengths, different talents worth noting. Some were definite marketing types, for example, and some definitely engineering types. The marketing gang was always big with ideas, but the engineers were constantly deflating their ideas by pointing out their potential constraints, making the ideas infeasible.

Angus remembered the old man and their near-accident with the guy who had cut them off that morning. He realized that the engineering types were not a band of bad guys out to sabotage everything. They were sincerely there to help and yet their tendency as engineers was to focus on distinctions and differences. It made them excellent engineers and scientists, but they were often difficult in team meetings. In their minds, they were making sure that ideas were backed with the specific technology to pull them off. Yet, without a specific time and place to submit their considerations, they became like Scud missiles, blowing up any creative idea that came along.

Angus realized that by asking them to reserve their considerations for specific agenda items that he would add to the meetings, he would be acknowledging and capitalizing on what they did well. He would be able to turn idea-puncturing skeptics into vital quality-control experts, thereby keeping the brainstorming sessions alive.

Within a few miles, Angus noticed some orange cones lined up in the right lane far ahead of him. He felt that old instinct rising up in him, the need to gripe about another rush-hour delay. But instead of his normal rant, he used this as an opportunity for a Centering Breath. Within seconds he became aware of another road sign: MERGE.

Another lesson! Everywhere I look I find my master teacher in disguise. Talk about asking for a sign!

Without question, the solution appeared, and it suddenly seemed so simple, and so doable.

My people are so talented. Discovering what they do best and then merging these distinct talents—that's my role—to serve them, not browbeat them into accepting my ideas.

Angus kept doing the Possibility Breathing, envisioning an aligned team, centered, creative, and energized. Over the next fifteen minutes, the particulars of a strategy to "yield" and "merge" began to flow in vivid detail.

Before Angus knew it, he had come to the busy intersection near his home, and as usual got "the red light from hell," as he called it, because it was long enough to make you feel guilty and still have time to get out your wallet for the homeless guy. Now, as if to prove his point, there was a fender-bender in the intersection and all traffic was at a standstill. But Angus now welcomed this "centering light," treasuring the opportunity to collect his thoughts. Time was no longer his opponent. He continued to let his mind flow, creating an environment for a *real* team to emerge.

Suddenly, Angus was riveted by the image in front of him. There was Eddy, the homeless guy who had always irritated him, who touched in Angus some dark-sided mixture of guilt and pain. Eddy worked his route from car to car, oblivious to the blinding snow and wind. Behind him, another yellow roadside sign on the curb read "SOFT SHOULDER." These words, in juxtaposition with Angus's hardened attitude regarding Eddy and his disenfranchised, marginalized sector of society ("Why don't they get a job and quit draining the country's resources?") shot an arrow into Angus's heart. His recognition of his own hard exterior, a self-imposed wall to avoid facing his own fear of failure, softly made its way to the surface, like a spring flower bursting out of rock and snow.

Angus squeezed into the lane where Eddy was working. The snow was falling in big, wet flakes. The car thermometer indicated it was a damp thirty degrees outside, and the wind was gaining force. Eddy was dressed in a beat-up cloth jacket and red hunter's cap, no gloves, and his jeans and ragged tennis shoes couldn't have offered much warmth. Yet he moved with his same deliberate pace, holding up his "I'm Eddy. Thank you for your help" sign, and carrying his large metal can. He didn't approach people directly unless they first engaged him with a look or by rolling down a window.

Eddy came toward him, and Angus took in a very conscious breath, letting in his highest self. He breathed in the power to get beyond the "story" that held him back, the "get a job" one that was full of judgment and hostility. Then, he rolled down his window.

"Pretty cold out there! Don't you have a place to get warm?"

"No, sir. I don't want to waste this rush-hour time. But I certainly appreciate your thoughts. Did you make it to work on time yesterday?"

Angus couldn't believe what he was hearing. "You remember me?"

"You sped by me pretty fast, remember?"

Everywhere I Look I Find

My Master Teacher

in Disguise

Angus felt shame and amazement simultaneously. He scrutinized Eddy: long, unkempt hair on the sides, balding on the top, gray beard, hunched back, gimpy knees, aged, weather-beaten face. If anybody needed a soft shoulder to lean on, it was this man. But his deep brown eyes had clarity and wisdom in them.

"Are you able to survive out here, doing this?" Angus knew immediately it was a stupid question.

"I'm still standing," Eddy drawled. "And the Lord keeps providing. These people driving by have helped out me and a lot of folks at our homeless shelter."

"You work for a shelter?"

"I work there and live there. I give them everything because they took me in and saved my life."

"Why don't you write on your sign that you are collecting for a shelter?"

"People'd never believe it. They'd think I was scamming like so many do on the streets. So I don't even try."

Angus dropped a twenty into the red can.

"Thank you, sir. You just never know when the blessings are going to show up."

"I feel the same way," Angus confessed.

He looked at Eddy, who was gazing back with kindness. Angus realized that somehow, in a split second, the roles had switched—Angus was the one who had been living the cold and isolated life, while Eddy lived the warm life of community, compassion, and purpose that Angus longed for.

"Does it get old being here every day?" Angus asked, trying to prolong the conversation.

"I get old!" laughed Eddy. "But life doesn't! There's always something going down out here."

The light changed and the traffic started to pull away.

Eddy let out a big toothless grin, tapped the top of the car, and moved on.

Angus plodded along through the raging snowstorm. *My life seemed so trapped and uninspiring. And then, today, miracle after miracle, learning after learning! Have these things, these people, always been there, just waiting to be discovered? What kept me from seeing?*

Again, Angus glanced at his face in the mirror. He knew the answer. It was just hard to admit. *All my righteous judgments of everything and everyone, that's what! I've been living in the past, having already pegged everyone into their slots.*

At the next red light Angus took a long hard look at the

Two Deep Breaths card on the dashboard. He stared into the snow-white night. Then it came to him—the Third Breath:

The Discovery Breath
Breathe in the Mystery,
let go of judgment

The Discovery Breath

∾

Breathe in the Mystery,

let go of judgment

THREE DEEP BREATHS

The Centering Breath

Breathe in the present moment,

with balance and energy

❧

The Possibility Breath

Breathe in the "me I want to be"

with power and purpose

❧

The Discovery Breath

Breathe in the Mystery,

let go of judgment

∾

The Mystery

Angus turned the car onto his home street. He drove slowly, trying to actually be present in his neighborhood rather than rushing through it. The heavy snow made the lights in the homes glow with a feeling of safety and warmth.

His eyes caught sight of the sign he had driven by every day for years:

SLOW: CHILDREN PLAYING

"There might be some wisdom in that for me!" chuckled Angus to himself.

He pulled into the driveway, and took a long look at his home. He took the first breath, the Centering Breath, and felt gratitude for his family. He took in the second breath, the Possibility Breath, and simply asked, "Let the highest level of me as parent and spouse show up." Then he took out a pen and added the third breath to the card on the dashboard.

When he opened the door, Carly rushed past him to leave.

"Sierra's eaten. She's doing homework. I'll be back around ten."

Angus remembered that this was Carly's weekly yoga class and dinner-with-the-girls night.

"See you then. Have fun."

He watched her as she hurried out. He wanted to say much more, but he knew it wasn't the right time.

He could see from the entryway that Sierra was in the TV room. He hung up his coat and went to her.

"Hi, Sierra! How's my girl?" He kissed her on the top of the head.

"Hi," grunted Sierra, without looking up at him. She was reading a schoolbook, chewing on a strip of licorice, and looking up periodically to check out a show on the television.

I have been training her too well, Angus thought. *There she is, multitasking just like me.*

"Doing homework?"

"Uh huh."

"I'm going to make some hot chocolate on this snowy night. Would you like some?"

"Sure." Sierra actually looked up at her father walking away. His behavior wasn't typical. Usually he'd go to his office and check his e-mails first, and then be preoccupied all night.

It wasn't long before Angus had made two steaming cups of hot chocolate and set them down with some crackers and cheese on the coffee table in the living room. He readjusted the couch so that it was facing the big bay window looking out at the snowstorm. He turned off the living room lights so they could see the heavy flakes falling softly under the streetlights.

"Hot chocolate's ready. Come and get it!"

Sierra looked up and noticed the darkness in the adjacent room.

"What are you doing?" she said, annoyed.

"I'm looking at the Mystery."

Sierra rolled her eyes at her dad. She wanted to say, "I'd rather drink my hot chocolate out here," but she found herself needing to find out what this strange behavior was all about.

Sierra walked into the living room and saw her father sipping hot chocolate in the dark, looking out at the storm.

"Wow!" she exclaimed and rushed to the window. "Look how much it's snowed! Everything's covered already."

Thank goodness she can drop her "stuff" and get present so quickly. She hasn't acquired all my bad habits!

Sierra plopped down on the couch, mesmerized by the storm. "Look at how the snow forms little 'hats' on the mailboxes and bushes," she said. "They look like a bunch of elves and hobbits playing!"

Angus looked and grew amazed. "You're right, Sierra! I see them! The whole yard is blessed with little friends celebrating winter!"

"Is this 'the Mystery,' Daddy?"

Angus looked at her. "That's sort of what I mean by the Mystery, Sierra. Yesterday I thought I knew everything. Today, I realize I have no idea. And just knowing that I don't have to know, makes me feel free and happier. Do you know what I mean?"

"I guess so." Sierra sipped from her hot chocolate, more interested in the snowfall than a philosophical discussion.

"Sierra, I am really sorry I missed another game."

"That's all right, Daddy." Her answer came automatically, as if she had spouted that line many times before. "And besides it got canceled because of the weather."

"Well, I want to apologize anyway." He wanted to tell her that he always had excuses. That this was his "story" and it kept him from being "the me" he wanted to be. He was tired of excuses and tired of keeping hidden who he really was. He loved her far more than any job or any excuses and he wanted to live a life that showed it.

Not quite sure how to express these feelings, Angus reached over and squeezed her hand.

"Sierra, I want to thank you for teaching me something very important!"

"What?" asked Sierra, looking inquisitively at her father.

"For telling me last night to find my teacher, and to be open for learning."

"Did you find your teacher?"

"Better than that. I found that everything I saw and listened to was my teacher. In disguise! All I had to do was give up what I thought I was seeing, and open up to the Mystery."

"Whatever," said Sierra, and Angus laughed.

"That's right!" he said. "Whatever!"

Then he gave a nod toward the snow.

"What is that out there? Is it frozen rain? Is it elf hats? Is it a day off from school, or an invitation to drink hot chocolate together?"

"How about a chance to make a snowman?" Sierra asked hopefully.

"Yes! Let's surprise Mom and put it on the front lawn!" Angus pumped his fist and Sierra laughed as they both jumped up off the couch.

Angus felt the snowball hit him square in the back as he

left the front porch. Bundled up like Eskimos, they chased each other around the yard like two puppies released from the kennel. Before long they were working like two crazed architects, changing plans by the minute, as the snowman began to emerge. A wastebasket for his top hat, an apple on a fork for his nose, licorice sticks for the mouth, blue coasters for the eyes, and four large precariously balanced snowballs for the body instead of three, because they had so much fun rolling them into creation.

Angus and Sierra stood arm in arm and admired their work. Sierra looked up at the sky and the falling snow.

"Isn't this neat? All this fun stuff just falls from the sky." Then she looked closely at the snowman and the snow falling all around them. "I guess the sky just throws down the good stuff. And then it's up to us to put it together and have fun with it."

"You're right, Sierra." Angus began to rethink the "stuff" that he had been given every day, from red lights to road signs, the old man, Daisy, and Eddy. How had he failed to see the gifts? He laughed out loud, staring into the night sky, holding out his hands.

"Snowmen fall from heaven unassembled."

He watched Sierra put her scarf around the snowman's neck. But it was he who felt warm, connected, and grateful.

Her teacher was right. The answers do come when we just look for them.

Sierra was already absorbed in something new, lying on her back in the snow.

"Come on, Daddy! Make a snow angel!"

Angus, on cue, held his arms straight out to his side, became stiff as a board, and plopped backwards into the snow. Sierra burst into laughter at the sight.

Snowmen Fall

from Heaven

Unassembled

Then he began waving his arms and legs in the snow.

Big flakes fell on their faces. They stuck out their tongues to catch them.

"Wow, that was a big one."

"That one was a double!"

"Do you notice how your eyes blink right before they get hit, even without your trying?"

Father and daughter, angels amidst God's stuff, laughed at the Mystery floating softly around them, on them, in them.

Sierra rose to her knees and studied her father lying flat on his back in the snow, staring into the vastness of black and white. Sierra traced once more the furrow on his brow running down toward his nose.

"Did you learn what to do about this, Daddy?"

"Is that old worry wrinkle still there?" he asked, feigning surprise and concern, making the furrow even deeper.

"I can still see it," Sierra answered.

"Well, then get some snow and rub it off!" Angus shouted.

Sierra grabbed a glove full of snow and rubbed it vigorously into his face and then pulled her hand away.

With a great big snowy smile, Angus looked up at her.

"How is it now? Has it changed?"

"It's gone!" yelled Sierra in a burst of laughter.

And then as if the world suddenly fit perfectly, Angus gave a loud joyous whoop and Sierra began rolling around in the snow.

Children playing.

The Journal

After he tucked Sierra in, Angus sat at his desk staring at the computer. He had a pile of e-mails, but they could wait. This day was too important to put on the back burner. He created for himself a new screen saver:

Three Deep Breaths

The Centering Breath
Breathe in the present moment,
with balance and energy

The Possibility Breath
Breathe in the "me I want to be"
with power and purpose

The Discovery Breath
Breathe in the Mystery,
let go of judgment

Angus looked at the Three Deep Breaths for quite some time. More than anything, he wanted to share this with

Carly. But how could he possibly explain the significance of
this day to her in a way she could understand? They hadn't
had an intimate conversation in months. Explaining it
to Carly felt far more difficult than sharing it with Sierra,
or even with his project team. He reread the words on the
screen. What would keep them from appearing trite—just
a bunch of words—to Carly? How could he explain that, to
him, they represented so much more: a daily practice that
could—and already had started to—change his life.

Angus pulled out a black leather journal from the back
of his desk drawer. Carly had given it to him several years
ago thinking that he might try keeping a journal as she had
been doing since her teenage years. Angus opened it for the
first time, the blank pages no longer threatening.

He reached for a small box on a shelf above his desk.
With a heart full of memories, he lifted out a pen—his late
father's gold fountain pen, awarded by his company "for
exemplary service." This was just the pen for this occasion.
Then he went over to the couch, propped up a couple of
pillows, and sat down. He opened the journal and began to
write his first entry ever.

Two hours later, when Carly walked in the front door,
Angus was watching the snow, which was still coming
down.

"You're not on the computer!" a startled Carly said. "Is
everything okay?"

"Everything is more than okay. Everything is miracu-
lous."

Carly took off her coat, without taking her eyes off Angus. There he was, basking in candlelight, two glasses and a
bottle of her favorite Pinot on the table.

And a snowman in the front yard.

She sat down close to him on the couch.

"How was your evening?" asked Angus with a grin, so large that you knew it contained a surprise.

"The usual—good workout, nice salad, and fun gossip. Obviously nothing as significant as what's been happening around here!"

Angus could not hold back now.

"Carly, do you remember when you were little, and you'd go on a trip to the beach with your parents? How exciting it was? You'd dig in the sand and get it all stuck to you, and then you'd run into the waves and they'd knock you down, and crash all over you, and you'd be all swirled around as the foam pushed you back up to the shore. And you'd be laughing, no—delirious—with the joy of being totally out of control and vulnerable. That's what it felt like to me today—all day."

"Are you okay? Did you get fired? Did you have an accident?" asked Carly, anxiously.

Angus put his hand on Carly's and smiled reassuringly.

"No. It's just that I had a realization. I realized that every moment is so special, just like a wave of its own. I don't want to miss them anymore, Carly."

Carly glanced at the bottle. It had not been opened. His intoxication must have come from something else. She nodded toward the snowman.

"Did you and Sierra do that?"

"What an absolutely wonderful daughter you've raised," Angus said.

"You mean *we've* raised!" laughed Carly. "I'm so happy you two had so much fun."

"Carly, I'm really sorry I've been so distant and unavailable for, well, for a long time."

Carly did not reply.

"I have no excuses. Only sadness."

"What happened? Why now?" Carly gestured to the darkness, the candlelight, the unopened wine. "Why this?"

"I wasn't sure I could explain it all," he ventured. Then Angus reached over and gently placed the journal in her lap.

"Sierra touched my wrinkled brow last night and asked me what it meant. I really had no idea. Until today. So I wrote this."

With trepidation laced with excitement, Carly ran her hands softly over the cover of the book. Then she slowly opened it.

I forgot how to breathe. I don't know when it began. Maybe when I was very little and I had a high fever and everything started to change size, and different geometric patterns would appear and zoom in and out. I was scared because I was losing control and I had learned that losing control somehow meant dying. Maybe it was when I had to stand up in front of the music class and sing, something people told me I was lousy at. Or when my father took me out into the deep end on his shoulders and he wouldn't bring me back to the side of the pool, insisting I be a man at the age of five. A thousand little things. It got harder and harder to breathe, to feel okay about myself. It became all about getting the A's or making the team so people would like me. It was all about what they thought—my teachers, my friends, my coaches—only with their approval could I breathe easy.

All those daily anxieties became excitement without breath. And what happened when the anxiety became big fear? No breath at all! Like when I was ten, sprinting full-out through the woods in the dark, the shortest way home from Donny's house. It was only two blocks, but it felt like eternity. I couldn't breathe for fear that I would wake up the Werewolf! Or find, when I opened the door to my dark bedroom and was met by my image in the full-length mirror, the ax killer himself!

Or asking Sharon to dance in junior high.

Yes, I guess I stopped breathing a little bit every day. And now I'm a master of not breathing, so good at it that most people wouldn't notice. I breathe, of course. I just don't breathe deeply. Just like I merely live, instead of living deeply.

My fear doesn't show itself like it used to, either. That would be too embarrassing. It's disguised in thousands of subtleties. I'm now highly skilled at putting the blame on Carly or Robert or Harold so my fear can stay hidden, while it secretly runs my life. I can't stomach one more notch against my performance or my approval rating. Fear keeps me stuck, judging everybody else around me so I can appear okay.

Fear wants me to dwell in the past or in the future. It doesn't want me to live in this present moment and become awake. Because fear can't live there. Because the present moment isn't fearful. If I stay angry over a disagreement with Carly, I'm stuck in the past. If I'm constantly obsessed over my job security, then I'm dwelling in the future. But when I turn on the light, the scary image in my bedroom becomes only me in the mirror. When I get present, and awake, fear dissolves.

So I've been holding my breath, and holding back my life. When I don't take time to play with Sierra because I'm so concerned about the future and the past, I am forgetting to breathe. When I don't notice Carly's beautiful essence, I am forgetting to breathe. When I don't appreciate the gift that each person is, I am forgetting to breathe. When I am unwilling to face my own fear and anxiety, I am forgetting to breathe.

Carly reached over to hold Angus's hand. Angus put her hand in both of his, as she read on.

Until I am willing to turn the light on, I will continue to need to be right at all costs. My need to be right has usurped my need to experience life. Everything I see and do goes through that filter, "Am I right? Am I okay?" I have a definite opinion about everything, everybody. And in my mind, I am brilliantly right about each one of those opinions, which only strengthens the bars of my imprisonment.

Well, I am fed up with who I have become. I'm like the Wizard of Oz, scared and cowardly and heartless, hiding behind some phony charade.

Last night Sierra said something so simple and yet so profound. "If you don't know something just ask your teacher." I always thought I knew everything. I had forgotten how to ask, and in my judgmental mind there was no room for a teacher. Until today. Today I didn't find one teacher, I found many. Today was like some miracle intervention: everywhere I looked was my master teacher in disguise: an old man in a '57 Chevy, the groundskeeper at my office, my boss, road signs, billboards, an aspen branch, and Eddy the homeless guy. And of course, Sierra.

I now find myself on a journey. I can see that it may be an arduous, long journey. It is a journey to be the me I want to be —my authentic self. I see that it is a warrior's journey because it will take courage, awareness, and discipline. And forgiveness. Because I will fall off the path many times. The old path I was on is a super-highway, with so many cars and so much speed it seems impossible to change lanes, much less get off. This new journey, though, is like bushwhacking a trail of my own— full of serious battles with my old fearful self. But, if I remember to breathe, to wake up, the signposts appear as needed.

To take in a Centering Breath. To breathe in calmness and balance and awareness. To listen truly to a bird rather than guess man's name for it. To appreciate the possibility that the millions of atoms that I take in when I inhale could be those same atoms that were taken in by Jesus or Buddha or Muhammad thousands of years ago. They could be that full of healing and compassion. Am I willing to breathe that in?

To take in a Possibility Breath. To ask, "What's my highest purpose at this moment, in this situation?" To see Robert not as my opponent but as my co-leader, and Harold not as an intimidating boss but as a friend who wants me to succeed. When I see Carly, to breathe in the possibility that I can love her as she is, not as I want her to be. To support her unconditionally on her path, knowing that it might diverge from mine—not only in little things, like where to go for dinner or what movie to see, but in the bigger things, like dreams and aspirations, her desire to sing her song. To hold her in such a manner that she can fly and not be held back. To be of such unconditional support that she has the courage to lift off and explore. And even when we are so mad at each other that we can't speak and are lying in bed with our backs to each other—to remember my highest purpose, and reach over and gently touch her, silently saying that this too will pass, and that the love will flow again, even if it only starts with a trickle.

And then, to take in a Discovery Breath, the one I understand least of all. To deeply breathe in the Mystery. When Sierra was born, and I saw her little head appear and she slid into my arms, that was the Mystery. When I looked into her eyes, and into Carly's, and at that moment knew that I knew nothing, that was the Mystery. That was absolute wonder, breathing in a precious moment. And that little baby girl was just there, the embodiment of wonder and miracle. That was the Mystery.

Carly looked up from the journal with tears in her eyes and squeezed Angus's hand.

"Remember how she would look at us when we held her?" she reminded Angus. "She would look not just at us, but all around the periphery of our faces, like she could see something we couldn't. Even a piece of lint on the carpet was great cause for a crawling journey—not just to look, but to touch, to taste, to smell, to be. She was in the Mystery. She *was* the Mystery."

"Sierra brought me into the Mystery tonight. She could see the elves and hobbits out there." Angus leaned in close to Carly and pointed to the yard. "Like that elf mailbox out there, and those hobbit bushes. See?"

Carly looked and laughed. She shook her head, enjoying the thought of the magical night Angus and Sierra must have had together.

"Maybe the magic is happening in me, too," she said softly to herself, and went back to the journal.

I am learning one simple truth: I don't know what a single thing is. Oh, I have my labels—like "this is a pen" and "I'm writing on this paper"—to try to explain things, which I guess is fine. But then I build up assumptions and feelings and beliefs, and an entire drama of my own making. It wouldn't be too bad, except that I begin to believe that my drama is the truth and not a dream. And I become defensive when it differs from another's drama, because if mine can't stay intact, I think I'll lose control and die. So my war begins.

And it escalates.

But what if I can just breathe in the Mystery? If I can ask myself, of all there is to know in this infinite universe, how much do I know? If I were to represent the percentage of what

I know as the space between my finger and my thumb—I couldn't make that gap small enough. That infinitesimally small piece of knowledge, in relation to the whole universe! The lunacy of spending so much time trying to be so right about so little!

I can breathe and laugh and let go of the struggle. Not knowing is a wonderful thing; it can set me free. I can consciously choose that my next action, my next words, can come from an intent to learn, rather than from an intent to defend.

Today was a day of wonders. And I, Angus—the type-A, late-for-the-meeting, fuming-at-the-red-light, no-time-for-the-soccer-game, can't-find-a-parking-space Angus—was open to the Mystery of it all! Oh, let me be mindful again and again. Let the red light remind me, and the doorknob, and the ducks in the park. Billboards. A homeless person on the street. Sierra's laugh.

Snowmen fall from heaven unassembled.

Why Spend So Much Time

Trying to Be So Right

About So Little?

Practice, Practice, Practice

Angus opened one eye slightly, so he would appear to still be asleep. He watched his daughter twirling and leaping beside his bed, singing and performing a "wake-up" dance. Last night she had promised him that, instead of an alarm clock, she would be his "wake-up fairy" and awaken him to a magical day.

He felt Carly's hand gently nudging him, making sure he wasn't missing a moment. He wasn't. Angus's joy in this moment was almost overwhelming, but he held it back so that he could prolong the show.

Softly, Sierra danced high on her toes, in her little pink nightgown, chanting as she made her way in circles around the room.

"Wake up! It's a magic day! Wake up! Get up and play!"

Angus feigned a big slow yawn, as good as any Rip Van Winkle. With a shout, Sierra leaped onto the bed and waved her pretend wand over her dad. At just the right moment, Angus growled to life and, just like a giant grizzly bear, he grabbed Sierra and then Carly, too. His girls squealed with delight, just as he knew they would.

"Absolutely the best wake-up call the world has ever

known!" Angus told Sierra. "I can feel the magic happening ... happening ... happening ..." He slowly sat up on the bed, as though he were rising from a grave—as if reenacting a miracle, a rebirth—bringing the girls to hysterics.

"And now," he announced, "I am AWAKE!" He grabbed the pillows and began playfully flinging them at Sierra as she squealed in delight.

By breakfast, things had returned to normal. Except that Angus was sitting at the table and eating with them, discussing the events of the day.

What a pleasure to have gotten up a little earlier than usual, thought Angus. *Even my shower was a delightful cleansing waterfall instead of the "late lane" anxiety. And how rewarding to set aside a few minutes of quiet time to simply sit and breathe. Not to do anything about my breathing but to just watch it, the ebb and flow of life force, and be present.*

On the inhalations Angus had felt like an ocean wave was washing over his body, bringing him energy and health. And on the exhalation, the wave would recede, back to the ocean, taking with it his tension and anxiety. A few minutes of time simply watching his breath, hearing his breath, and visualizing its life force, was so simple to do. So relaxing. He wondered how he could have been so busy that he let himself miss this for so long. It was not like some stoic discipline, but natural, just like eating or sleeping. He realized that he wanted this to be a regular practice that he could do each day.

Angus suddenly looked at his watch, and his old anxiety hooked him again.

"Uh-oh. I have to leave!"

He jumped up, grabbed his coat and jacket, hugged his

girls, and bolted out the door. Just as he was in the car, the cell phone rang.

"Hi, Kelly. What? No way! That idiot! He can't do that! Tell him I want to meet him in my office as soon as I get in. No excuses!"

Angus slammed the cell phone shut. He angrily grabbed his seat belt and clicked it solid. The click exploded in his mind like a clap of thunder. He froze, and then stared down at the silver buckle around his belly.

"Centering Belt," he whispered softly, and then, as if he needed to hear it again and more distinctly, "Centering Belt."

He looked at the Three Deep Breaths on his dashboard.

"I can see this is going to be a long journey."

Slowly and consciously, Angus took Three Deep Breaths.

And then he redialed Kelly's number.

THREE DEEP BREATHS

The Centering Breath

Breathe in the present moment,

with balance and energy

～

The Possibility Breath

Breathe in the "me I want to be"

with power and purpose

～

The Discovery Breath

Breathe in the Mystery,

let go of judgment

Afterword

For many years, I have begun each day with a session of meditation and breathing exercises. It began as a discipline, an important part of my personal training regimen as a teacher of meditation and the martial arts. Now it is as natural and enjoyable as eating and sleeping, and as valuable. I think of my breathing as the fundamental source of nutrition for my mind and body, prior to even food or drink. I feel this daily practice is a most precious gift, because when I breathe deeply with awareness, every cell of my being gets packed with life force, vitality, and healing. My daily worries and trials melt into a new—and more joyful—perspective of lessons and opportunities. Who wouldn't want such a gift?

I have come to understand that most of our lives are so busy today that it is difficult to add one more thing to our already full plates. And for those of us who have some form of regular practice that produces stress reduction and well-being, we still have trouble integrating it into our daily lives. Have you ever exited your peaceful, inspiring yoga class only to find yourself raging at the slow-moving traffic? I wrote this parable to help both those people who have "no time" to establish a practice, and those who already have a practice but are looking for ways to integrate it more fully into their lives.

I believe there is an Angus in all of us—someone so needy for approval and so full of judgment than an entire day (or life) can be consumed by perceived competition and the obsession with doing that we multitask our way right out of the present moment. How do we find our way back home in today's world?

The way back home is profound, yet simple—only a few conscious breaths away. Right in the moment, even in the heat of anger or upset, the first breath can calm and soothe your body, the second breath can restore the tranquility of your mind, and the third breath can reunite you with the spirit. Just as Angus used stoplights, billboards, and door-knobs, you can identify your own cues to help you remember the Three Deep Breaths. As the old man said, "It doesn't take time, it takes intention." In fact, it will save time, and help you perceive time and stressful situations not as problems to be managed but as opportunities to connect with your joy and well-being.

And how about those people around you who need some support—mentally, physically, or spiritually—but don't have the courage to ask for it, or aren't yet open to new possibilities? Just being the centered model that you are by practicing and embodying Three Deep Breaths, you will be of great support. By allowing your full authentic self to show up, you can be a bridge to reach those people. With your first Centering Breath, you choose to be more centered and present, allowing yourself to be a great listener with compassionate presence. With the Possibility Breath, you use appreciative inquiry to help them discover their highest purpose and to live out of it. And with the Discovery Breath, you create an environment of non-judgment, supporting them in letting go of any resentment, guilt, and resistance that might hold them back from their own joy and fulfillment.

I offer *Three Deep Breaths* as a book to be practiced, as an approach to bring balance, purpose, and power into our lives.

In the past thirty years, there have been well over two thousand peer-reviewed studies of mind/body medicine, as well as writings by leading researchers in the field, such as Herbert Benson, Gregg Jacobs, and Ellen Langer of Harvard, Robert Sapolsky of Stanford, Richard Davidson of the University of Wisconsin, and Paul J. Rosch of the American Institute of Stress, to name a few. They show us that mind/body techniques like the Three Deep Breaths, which focus on proper breathing, deep relaxation, and mindfully choosing our perspectives, can actually bring balance to our autonomic nervous system. Their research reinforces the work of the many brilliant teachers throughout history who have shown us that mind/body processes can be far more valuable than any symptom-treating pill for suffering and stress. I am grateful to all who have contributed to this body of knowledge.

It is my hope that in reading *Three Deep Breaths* you will find support for becoming the best you that you can possibly be. After all: "Snowmen fall from heaven unassembled —it's up to us to put them together."

Thomas Crum

About the Author

Thomas Crum is an internationally known author, seminar leader, and martial artist. He leads workshops and trainings for organizations and major corporations throughout the world, including former hot spots such as the Soviet Union, Northern Ireland, and South Africa. He had the fortune of co-leading a session in Indonesia with the Dalai Lama.

Tom is the author of *Journey to Center* and *The Magic of Conflict* (both published by Simon and Schuster), as well as many audio and video products dealing with conflict, stress management, and peak performance. He is a unique "experiential" keynote presenter, with engagements at many international conferences and associations, including the American Society for Training and Development (ASTD), the American Management Association, Franklin Covey, the Ken Blanchard Companies, Systems Thinking in Action, National Speakers Bureau, and the Global Institute for Leadership Development.

Tom is founder and president of Aiki Works, Inc. (also d.b.a. Thomas Crum Associates), through which he offers a wide variety of programs to support individuals and organizations—from keynote addresses to multi-day trainings. His Magic of Conflict program, designed to help turn conflict into successful relationships, has supported thousands of employees at all levels of management in corporations, government, and nonprofit organizations. His most recent contribution to the workplace is his Three Deep Breaths workshop, which focuses on turning stress into vitality, pressure into power, and busy-ness into being.

Tom's work is applicable not only to the workplace, but also to every aspect of our lives—such as relationships, family, and athletic performance. The Journey to Center workshop is a five-day intensive training held each fall in Colorado. It aims to help individuals and teams to deeply integrate the work into every aspect of their lives, especially relationships. And for those among us who like to ski or play golf, Tom hosts residential programs in his hometown of Aspen, Colorado, integrating his work with these outdoor sports. The Magic of Skiing workshops are conducted with the Aspen Skiing Company each winter. In the summer, Tom hosts the Magic of Golf workshop with his son, Dr. Eric Crum, former captain of the Stanford University golf team.

A former systems analyst with a B.S. in mathematics from Bucknell University, Tom was a teacher and director of the Aspen Community School, a humanistic charter school for grades K–8. He co-founded the Aspen Academy of Martial and Healing Arts and has taught meditation and the graceful martial art of aikido, which optimizes the use of energy, focus, and balance, for over thirty years.

With singer/songwriter John Denver, Tom co-founded the Windstar Project, an educational center dedicated to environmental sustainability and the peaceful resolution of conflict. He served as executive director of that foundation from 1979 to 1985.

Tom and his wife, Cathy, live in the Rocky Mountains of Colorado, where they have raised three children.

For more information on Thomas Crum and his products and programs, please visit his website, www.thomascrum.com, or contact him through Aiki Works, Inc.

Aiki Works, Inc.
Tom@aikiworks.com

P.O. Box 7845
Aspen, CO 81612
970-925-7099

P.O. Box 251
Victor, NY 14564
585-924-7302

About Berrett-Koehler Publishers

Berrett-Koehler is an independent publisher dedicated to an ambitious mission: Creating a World that Works for All.

We believe that to truly create a better world, action is needed at all levels—individual, organizational, and societal. At the individual level, our publications help people align their lives with their values and with their aspirations for a better world. At the organizational level, our publications promote progressive leadership and management practices, socially responsible approaches to business, and humane and effective organizations. At the societal level, our publications advance social and economic justice, shared prosperity, sustainability, and new solutions to national and global issues.

A major theme of our publications is "Opening Up New Space." They challenge conventional thinking, introduce new ideas, and foster positive change. Their common quest is changing the underlying beliefs, mindsets, and structures that keep generating the same cycles of problems, no matter who our leaders are or what improvement programs we adopt.

We strive to practice what we preach—to operate our publishing company in line with the ideas in our books. At the core of our approach is *stewardship*, which we define as a deep sense of responsibility to administer the company for the benefit of all of our "stakeholder" groups: authors, customers, employees, investors, service providers, and the communities and environment around us.

We are grateful to the thousands of readers, authors, and other friends of the company who consider themselves to be part of the "BK Community." We hope that you, too, will join us in our mission.

Be Connected

Visit Our Website

Go to www.bkconnection.com to read exclusive previews and excerpts of new books, find detailed information on all Berrett-Koehler titles and authors, browse subject-area libraries of books, and get special discounts.

Subscribe to Our Free E-Newsletter

Be the first to hear about new publications, special discount offers, exclusive articles, news about bestsellers, and more! Get on the list for our free e-newsletter by going to www.bkconnection.com.

Participate in the Discussion

To see what others are saying about our books and post your own thoughts, check out our blogs at www.bkblogs.com.

Get Quantity Discounts

Berrett-Koehler books are available at quantity discounts for orders of ten or more copies. Please call us toll-free at (800) 929-2929 or email us at bkp.orders@aidcvt.com.

Host a Reading Group

For tips on how to form and carry on a book reading group in your workplace or community, see our website at www.bkconnection.com.

Join the BK Community

Thousands of readers of our books have become part of the "BK Community" by participating in events featuring our authors, reviewing draft manuscripts of forthcoming books, spreading the word about their favorite books, and supporting our publishing program in other ways. If you would like to join the BK Community, please contact us at bkcommunity@ bkpub.com.

PRODUCED BY WILSTED & TAYLOR PUBLISHING SERVICES
Copyediting by Nancy Evans
Design and composition by Yvonne Tsang